GODSPEED

GODSPEED

RACING IS MY RELIGION

L. D. Russell

continuum

NEW YORK • LONDON

2007

The Continuum International Publishing Group Inc
80 Maiden Lane, New York, NY 10038

The Continuum International Publishing Group Ltd
The Tower Building, 11 York Road, London SE1 7NX

www.continuumbooks.com

Copyright © 2007 by L. D. Russell

Portions of this book have appeared in the *Independent Weekly* and on the
Hillsborough Historical Society Web page.

Printed in the United States of America

Library of Congress Cataloging-in-Publication Data

Russell, L. D. (Larry Dean), 1955–
    Godspeed : racing is my religion / L.D. Russell.
        p.   cm.
    Includes bibliographical references.
    ISBN-13: 978-0-8264-1609-4 (pbk. : alk. paper)
    ISBN-10: 0-8264-1609-8 (pbk. : alk. paper)
    1. Stock car racing—United States.   2. Sports—Religious aspects—
Christianity.   3. NASCAR (Association)   I. Title.
GV706.42R87   2007
796.72—dc22
                                                              2007008492

Dedicated to my fallen heroes:
Dale Earnhardt, 1951–2001
Albert Leroy Wilson, 1921–1979

Wherefore seeing we also are compassed about with so great a cloud of witnesses, . . . let us run with patience the race that is set before us.

—Hebrews 12:1, King James Version

Do you not know that they who run a race all compete, but only one receives the prize? So run that you may win.

—1 Corinthians 9:24, my translation

I have fought the good fight, I have finished the race, I have kept the faith.

—2 Timothy 4:7, Revised Standard Version

CONTENTS

CONTENTS

ACKNOWLEDGMENTS

I wish to thank Henry Carrigan, my editor and dear friend from way back there in seminary school; my brothers, Frank, who taught me that courage means fleeing forward, and James, fellow survivor of the Bristol infield; my favorite ex-wife and best friend, Mary Lou Rollins, whose rockitude knows no bounds; Ed Holm, who accompanied me on the pilgrimage; Amy Beth Hildreth Hart, who loved me, loved me not; Bill Crowther, trustee of Ayr Mount Historical Site and guardian angel of Occoneechee Speedway; Alasdair MacIntyre, who gave me a safe place to practice my calling; my colleagues at Duke University and Elon University, who have shown such deep respect; my beloved students, who have taught me so much; and every kind soul who lit a candle on my behalf, especially those empathetic enough not to ask how the writing was coming along.

CHAPTER ONE

A Force of Nature

During the Daytona 500, opening race of NASCAR's 2001 season, I was doing two of my favorite things: writing at my computer and listening to the radio so I could pull for my working-class hero, Dale Earnhardt. After several near misses, Dale had finally won this Super Bowl of racing in 1998 on his twentieth try. Daytona was, they said, his Achilles' heel. As soon as he crossed the finish line that year, he spun donuts through the infield grass in his black and red #3 Chevy before slowing down to receive handshakes and high fives from all the other drivers and their mechanics, his fiercest competitors, who had poured out of the pits to congratulate him on his way to Victory Lane.

When the green flag dropped at Daytona in 2001 and the engines roared like angry hornets from my stereo speakers, I looked up at the framed photo of my grandfather, Papa Wilson, and blew his stubbly cheek a kiss. Grease monkey that he was, Papa planted the seed of stock car racing in my innocent soul. As a child, I listened to the races on the car radio while he worked on his '63 Impala. Papa always rooted for Fireball Roberts, an early stock car champion who drove hell-bent for leather until he was killed, ironically enough, in a fiery crash at Charlotte.

Zeroing in on the last few laps of the 2001 race, I ignored the computer and stared intently out the window at winter-bare trees as thirty drivers—all the ones who were left after a spectacular mid-race wreck had taken out a dozen or so cars—jockeyed at breakneck speeds for the money and the glory. You know the story: As the final lap came around, Earnhardt created a bottleneck so his son Dale Jr. and Michael Waltrip, both driving cars belonging to Dale Sr., could battle it out for the win. He never saw them cross the finish line.

Mom called early in the evening to tell me Dale had died of injuries suffered in the last-lap crash. A hush fell on my soul, the deep sense of shock and resignation that comes whenever I sense that the world has changed, and will never be quite the same. I phoned my dad, figuring if his firm voice couldn't stop my tears, nothing would. Long conversations with my brothers and a couple of racing buds helped it all finally begin to sink in. My grandfather never got over the loss of his favorite driver. After Fireball died, racing was just not the same. Papa still tuned in his radio every Sunday, but he didn't cuss and fume nearly as much. Now I know how he felt.

THE following Sunday, I met my brother James and one of his pals, Scott, at the North Carolina Speedway in Rockingham, the track known affectionately as the Rock. Scott had never been to a stock car race, and it's always fun to see someone catch the fever. I could tell by the fire in his eyes this was a longtime dream come true. James and I both remembered our first race, the Rebel 400 back in 1965, and we were just happy to witness his initiation.

It was the biggest funeral I've ever attended, the sky low and gray and full to bursting. Thousands of fans dressed in black, Dale's color of choice, packed the stands, and all around us were hats, T-shirts, and flags emblazoned with the number 3. After the national anthem was sung, Darrell Waltrip, a veteran driver from an earlier generation, said the opening prayer with a broken voice, assuring all that Dale was at peace in heaven. *At peace maybe,* I thought, *but how could the pearly gates hold such a force of nature?* When the starter waved his green flag and the cars all roared to full speed, I could hardly see them flash past for the tears in my eyes. As that old moonshine runner turned race car driver Junior Johnson had said, everybody at the Rock will know that "Earnhardt ain't in that race, and that's gonna hurt a little while."

The track was still damp from the morning's showers, and there was a nasty wreck before the first lap was through. Dale Jr. got bumped from behind and hit the wall much like his father had done just a week earlier, though at a slower speed. He climbed out and walked away from his mangled car, and everyone breathed again. After fifty laps in strengthening rain, the race was postponed until the next day. I wrapped my grief tenderly, as I would a family heirloom, and tucked it away.

The three of us partied at our campsite that evening, crazy with sorrow and a desperate desire to drink life to the very dregs. Grilled steak and a cold salad never tasted so good. We didn't speak of Dale, but his presence was heavy on us like the night dew. One of the strongest taboos in many cultures is to leave the dead unburied. It was as if Dale's spirit was still wandering the world in search of a place to rest.

Fortunately the gods smiled, and the next day dawned clear and crisp, one of those Carolina mornings so perfectly divine my muscles yearned to run and skip like a yearling colt. The race was run, and at about the midway point, Jeff Gordon was a straightaway ahead of the rest of the pack. Gordon is the youngblood who had threatened recently to steal Dale's racing crown in the same way Dale had swiped it years ago from the aging legend Richard Petty. But Steve Park, driving another of Earnhardt's cars, pulled off a maneuver that if Dale didn't invent he certainly perfected. At 150 mph he eased up behind Gordon and tapped his bumper just hard enough to make him let off the accelerator to keep from losing control, then powered around him to take the lead.

All too ironically, it was a bumper tap applied a little too hard at speeds a bit too fast that cost Dale his life. Nevertheless, such electric moments are the rush that racing fans live for. Park dominated the rest of the race, but toward the end Bobby Labonte, the driver who edged out Dale for 2000's NASCAR season championship, made a charge and finally caught Park on the last lap. They scraped fenders, and it was if the world stood still. When they came barreling out of the last turn, the crowd roared as Earnhardt's car pulled ahead to take the checkered flag. I threw both arms in the air, three fingers on each hand extended, and yelled out my joy and my sorrow. That moment felt for all the world like a small victory over death, a celebration of life, and a recognition of the thin line that separates them, for those who loved Dale and those who loved to hate him, and perhaps even for those who didn't understand him or what he was doing.

In the weeks that followed, I was more than a little surprised to find that my grief was shared by millions of other Americans. I had stopped at a red light, and in the rear window of the late-model SUV in front of me, I noticed what has become one of the most popular stickers in the history of the automobile, now an American icon: Earnhardt's slanted, red, white, and black #3. Beneath it was another sticker with the same #3 wearing white wings, Earnhardt's birth and death years, and the motto "Gone to Race in a Better Place." How's that for religion and racing?

In the past half century, stock car racing has mushroomed from its humble outlaw beginnings, southern Appalachian bootleggers in souped-up sedans outrunning revenuers at night and racing each other around cow pastures on weekend afternoons, to a multibillion-dollar enterprise commanding a weekly television audience in the millions and offering seven-figure purses. Shade-tree mechanics turning greasy wrenches on modified family cars have given way to college-educated technicians wielding the latest advances in aerodynamic engineering to push the envelope of speed and safety.

Ironically, it was Earnhardt's death, the widespread mourning that followed, and the press attention this phenomenon created that marked the coming of age of stock car racing and helped secure its place at the center of our national sports arena. I cannot count the number of friends and colleagues who had never before expressed any interest whatsoever in racing but who now asked me, because they knew I was a NASCAR fan, what all the hoopla was about. Needless to say, I was more than happy to tell them.

There was a time in the early 1990s when I would sit and wait until the very end of ESPN's Sunday night *SportsCenter* to catch the highlights of that day's race squeezed into a one- or two-minute blurb, a few sound bites and brief video clips of a wreck, the winner crossing the finish line, and beer baptizing a rejoicing pit crew in the winner's circle. Week after week, the commentators could not get through their coverage without affecting a smirking Southern accent and making a point of closing their comments with a juvenile wisecrack on the finishing position of their "favorite" driver, a man with the unfortunate name of Dick Trickle.

Now, of course, all that has changed. Stock car racing is bringing in the big bucks, and money talks. The Daytona 500 gets first billing on most sports reports across the country, and there are untold half-hour and full-hour shows dedicated solely to stock car racing and the drivers who have become press darlings, the American pop culture version of secular sainthood. A recent cover article in the *Spectator*, an entertainment newsweekly out of

Raleigh, North Carolina, was entitled "Hunks on Wheels: How the Most Redneck Sport Became Sexy." Written by a female fan and accompanied by a cover photo of Dale Earnhardt Jr., surely one of America's most eligible bachelors, the piece turned out to be a kind of primer for local high-society debutantes on how to secure a "trophy date" with one of stock car racing's handsome young studs. Apparently speed is not the only thrill to be gained from going to the races. There's competition, and then there's competition.

So why is it that millions of Americans are turning from their traditional allegiances to baseball, football, and basketball to follow the racing circuit? The excitement is obvious, as are the pageantry, the glamour, and the money, but there is also something else, a deeper force at work here, if only we have eyes to see. Stock car racing, with all its danger and daring, touches a nerve in the American psyche. Ours is a culture fascinated by death and starved in our guts for immortality. How many billions of dollars do we spend each year looking for ways to look and feel younger, to slow if not halt the aging process? How many simulated deaths occur on television and in movie theaters every single night of the week? We as viewers participate in these untimely ends, as if we might gain a foretaste of our own demise, a glimpse of what surely lies ahead for each and every one of us.

Anyone brave or crazy enough to dare death, to place themselves purposefully in danger's way, somehow gives us hope that we might have alternatives to simply giving up and succumbing to the inevitable march of time. A noble, courageous death is the next best thing to rolling away the stone from the mouth of the tomb. Stock car racing may not offer eternal life, but the inherent danger of the sport, its weekly flirtation with death, surely grants its fans, whether they realize it or not, a deep sense of comfort and courage this side of the Great Unknown.

Just in case you think my focus on driving, danger, and death is the product of paranoia: After writing the above passage, I took a break and drove thirty miles to buy my hard-to-find brand of cigarettes at an interstate outlet in the next town. Listening to public radio on the way over, my ears perked up at a news story on the worst storm to hit Memphis, Tennessee, in one hundred years, blowing the roofs off houses and felling trees by the dozens. It reminded me of my lifelong wish to see a tornado, that deadly freak of nature I have heard described as the finger of God, an image of chaos that seeks me out in my dreams. I'm no storm chaser, mind you. The ideal vantage point would be to witness a twister from a safe distance, not up close and personal.

What I didn't know as I drove out Highway 54, one of those classic two-lane country roads rolling along the low hills of the Carolina Piedmont, was that the same storm system, a cold front blowing through the midsummer heat, had killed several people across the Midwest and was now raking its way across central North Carolina. The horizon was gray and heavy when I arrived at the outlet, and by the time I climbed in my truck for the ride back home, dark clouds hung low overhead. Just as I took the exit off the interstate highway for the last twenty-minute leg of my trip through the country, jagged lightning bolts split the sky ahead and thunderclaps rolled across the surrounding fields. Fat raindrops splashed against the windshield, so I rolled up the window, turned on the wipers and headlights, and slowed to well below the speed limit. Heading down into a creek valley, my two-ton truck rocked to one side as it was struck by sudden gusts of wind. The nearby trees bent back and forth, and the temperature dropped at least ten degrees. I sat up straight and gripped the steering wheel with both hands just before a whirl of rainwater rolled right up the road at me and engulfed the truck. Blinded for a long moment, I tapped the brake pedal to slow without skidding, praying silently that no cars were headed my way either from the front or behind. The wind grew stronger, but the rain slacked up briefly before pounding my roof again even harder. Tree limbs lay scattered across the road ahead, and I kept an eye out for hail. *Surely*, I thought, *there's a twister out there somewhere.*

Three times I pulled off into roadside parking lots when the rain fell so hard I could not see. Each time, things cleared up, and I would pull back out into traffic, emergency flashers going, yet before long the hard rain would come again to force me off the road. For several miles I drove through an open area surrounded by fields full of tasseled corn, and the sky was as ominous as I have ever seen it, slanted angles of dark rain and lightning flashes across the distance, grayish clouds speeding along beneath the heavy black blanket above. The air held an odd color, sickening yellowish green, and there was a spark to it, a weird energy that put my senses on edge and pushed me to listen for the infamous roar of a freight train, the surest sign that the finger of God has found you.

I did not see a twister, and I must say I am not disappointed. What I did encounter, just after the sky finally brightened a bit and the rain slowed to a drizzle, was another pickup truck off the near side of the road, its hood and fenders smashed from having just rear-ended a small sedan whose trunk was folded up like a race car that has smacked the wall backwards at high speed. Other travelers had stopped to help, so I drove slowly on, thinking to myself (and feeling guilty for thinking it because those fellow travelers could not share the sentiment), *There but for the grace of God. . . .*

Thirty minutes after arriving back home, my insides were still shaking.

CHAPTER TWO

Speed Demons
and Daredevils

On a hot and sunny weekday morning, I walked into the woods with two other men. How was I to know we were stepping into the past? Bill Crowther, trustee of the Ayr Mount Historical Site, which now includes the old Hillsborough Occoneechee Speedway grounds, led the way, and Charlie Burger, a landscape architect who was studying to become a deacon in the Byzantine Catholic Church, followed close behind. We trudged along a bumpy, grass-covered trail all grown over with blackberry bushes and seedling pines. Bill and Charlie spoke of plans to restore the site and their desperate fight with the town fathers and the Department of Transportation to block construction of a planned bypass that would have run right over the raceway if not for Ayr Mount's intervention. The deeper into the forest we walked, the quieter our voices grew until we could hear only our footsteps, hushed by the tall grass, and the distant swoosh of traffic.

When the trail split, we bore to the right and suddenly we were standing in the first turn of the Occoneechee Speedway, looking right down the barrel of the front stretch. But if I hadn't been told this was a raceway,

I'm not sure I would have known. It looked for all the world like an old wagon trail, carpeted with grass except for the deep ruts, bedrock showing through in the bare spots. Crickets were raising Cain over in the infield, and a bright red cardinal chased its brownish mate through the low-hanging branches of a huge oak. I could not imagine the Flock boys and that madman Curtis Turner racing here.

But then something happened, what to my mind is a mystical experience, as if I had slipped into a time warp. I heard the growl of a tractor-trailer truck out on nearby Interstate 85, followed close behind by the unmistakable, throaty roar of a Harley, and the muscles of my legs and back tensed to leap out of the way of thirty-odd bellowing beasts, big Fords, Chevies, and Chryslers sprouting fins like dragon wings, as they stampeded down the straightaway and slid sideways to round the turn where we stood like deer mesmerized on the highway. I could smell the burning fuel, could almost taste the grease and dust. The pits were a hornet's nest of flashing wrenches and twirling tire irons. Across the way, a frenzied multitude of yahoos stood on their feet and screamed bloody murder. *Oh yeah*, I thought to myself, *this is where it all began.*

I jumped when Bill said, "Let's head down to the river."

We walked along the banked curves of turns one and two, and as my vision faded, I said, "Hey, let's go get the trucks and give 'em a spin. Once for old time's sake."

Charlie laughed and pointed to an oak fallen like a road-block across the second turn.

When we topped the rise and started down the hill toward the water, I saw in my mind an old black-and-white photo of Bobby Isaac's 1962 #99 Plymouth flying over this very banking on its way to the river below. *Those were crazy times,* I thought, *and even crazier men, but thank God for 'em!* The Eno River flowed lazily by as it has for thousands of years, long eons before two-legged animals first roamed these woods. Minnows scampered around gnarled roots and smooth rocks near the water's edge. A bright green dragonfly perched on a quivering branch. Beneath the shallow current, I could just make out an old tire, a proud veteran of the racing wars, now a condominium for catfish. Rusting on the riverbank was a drink box, as big and bulky as a casket, with *Pepsi-Cola* scrolled across the side.

ALTHOUGH racing and religion have long been joined at the hip, their relationship has not always been a happy one. In fact, these two cultural forces started off more as enemies than as friends. Or maybe it's closer to the truth to say that like Jacob and Esau, those contentious brothers of old, theirs was a sibling rivalry.

The earliest days of stock car competition saw a long-running battle between racing and religion, a series of skirmishes and full frontal assaults not far from the buckle of the Bible Belt and only a stone's throw from stock car racing's throbbing heart, in the ancient rolling hills of the North Carolina Piedmont. It was September 1947 when the *News of Orange County* announced on its front page that Bill France and four other promoters were planning to build a one-mile oval racetrack just outside the tiny town of Hillsboro, North Carolina. The National Association of Stock Car Auto Racing (NASCAR) itself would not be organized for a couple more months, Darlington Raceway had not yet been built, and the speedway at Daytona was still half beach sand and half coastal highway. The new Hillsboro track would become only the third mile-oval raceway on the Eastern seaboard, just about midway between the other tracks in Atlanta, Georgia, and Langhorne, Pennsylvania. The grandstands were to seat a total of five thousand spectators.

France and his partners purchased the outlying fields of the old Occoneechee farm so that they could tuck their new dirt track into an oval bend in the Eno River, where Carolina red clay was packed down over solid bedrock. They even used the straightaways of a horse track that had stood on the site in days gone by, a lasting testament to the age-old human need for speed that far outdates the invention of the automobile. By the summer of '48, the Occoneechee Speedway was ready to rock, and on Sunday, June 27, Fonty Flock, who went on to win that year's national championship, took the checkered flag with an average speed of nearly seventy-five miles per hour. Flock and his brothers, Bob and Tim, wasted no time establishing a monopoly at the track, winning almost every feature event during its first two seasons of operation. Chasing Fonty Flock that dusty day were other drivers who made names for themselves as the pioneers of stock car racing: Curtis Turner, Buddy Baker, and Glen "Fireball" Roberts.

The track caught on like wildfire. Within two years, amid rumors of what would soon become the Korean War, the races at Occoneechee Speedway were attracting fifteen thousand fans. Most came to see the best and fastest drivers, but like Shakespeare's groundlings, the common folk who showed up more for the circus sideshow than for the play, many were drawn to the track by promotional gimmicks. For instance, Wendell Scott, a black man from Danville, Virginia, with little or no backing and a bellyful of courage, competed against racial prejudice both on and off the track. And Louise Smith was the first (but by no means the only) woman entry at the track, running in the fall race of 1950. She turned out to be more than just fluff, giving the good ol' boys a good run for their money.

However, not everyone in and around Hillsboro was excited about this "double feature thrill program" and the rowdy behavior that came along with it. The lines of battle between religion and racing were being drawn. Already two years earlier the Orange County Council of Churches had convinced the county board of commissioners to ban the sale of beer on Sundays, and by 1950 the local press was giving more and more attention to the dangers of speeding and the horrors of automobile accidents. Most of these wrecks involved the deadly but all too common combination of drinking and reckless driving.

By August 1950, the Hillsboro commissioners, "unanimously expressing alarm over the use of certain streets as virtual speedways . . . moved to apply corrective measures to bring the situation under control." The town was ordered to put up a stoplight and lower the speed limit from thirty-five to twenty-five. In September of that year, the front page of the *News of Orange County* carried an article on the local traffic court handing out heavy fines and even time on the chain gang to youths caught racing each other and the police through the countryside. Nearby was another article detailing the annual increase in deaths and injuries due to car wrecks. Tucked in between was a headline: "Second Race of Season Sunday at Occoneechee." Tickets cost all of two dollars for the infield and three dollars for the grandstands, yet the reporter could not have helped racing's fledgling cause in the eyes of its religious opponents when he referred to the drivers as "speed demons."

The *News* fired its own volley across racing's bow in an October editorial reacting to a recent grisly automobile accident in which an unidentified convertible, described by an eyewitness as "doing all it could," lost control and slammed into an oncoming tractor-trailer truck. Five occupants of the car were killed and two were injured, one seriously. The editor went on to sermonize about the deadly dangers of "speeding and indifference to the serious business of driving." From here it was a small step to connect the furious pace of race cars on the track to speeding sports cars on the highways.

That connection, long since made by law-abiding local citizens, became public in April 1956. The Sunday race crowds had increased steadily, and the winning purse had grown from one thousand dollars in 1949 to forty-six hundred dollars. At a time when Senator Joseph McCarthy was stirring up anti-Communist, Red Scare hysteria, the Reverend W. I. Conway, pastor of the Gospel Baptist Tabernacle, declared war on the local racing enthusiasts. Going before the county commissioners to protest the construction of another racetrack, which promised to feature Sunday "jalopy races" only a half mile—about the length of a straightaway—from his church sanctuary, Rev. Conway branded such racing as "legalized murder."

Conway gained a sympathetic hearing at the board meeting, along with a loud amen from a *News* editorial citing "highway racing and the mania for speed which seems to possess many of our generation." Because the planned races would allow only amateur drivers in older model cars, the writer said, "We would point the finger of shame at such irresponsibility." Whether or not he realized it, the editorialist's closing words echoed the fears of many Americans expecting an imminent Communist invasion of our shores: "We appeal to our public officials, we appeal to public opinion to take a firm stand for sanity and smother this menace to our safety and that of our neighbors before it gains further foothold in our midst."

Such antiracing fervor soon gained momentum when Presbyterian minister Rev. C. H. Reckard (pronounced "wreck hard") joined the fray. "We have not done right by our children," he wrote in an April 1956 *News* op-ed piece. "We have allowed two racetracks to be constructed in our community, the least concern of which is the disruption of our Sundays and the worst a stimulation of our young people to excessive and daring driving and the exposing of them to public drinking and gambling." So there it was, a trinity of evils: recklessness, intoxication, and gambling, and all on the Lord's own day.

The next month, Rev. Conway opened the doors of his Gospel Tabernacle to host a "mass meeting" that turned out to be a kind of antiracing revival service. As he had done before the commissioners, Conway once again drew a connection between "the present highway accident trend" and "the racing mania." The *News* ran its report of this meeting just beneath a photograph showing the proper and acceptable role for young men: a line of Boy Scouts in full uniform emblazoned with merit badges.

The total attendance at the church meeting came to around one hundred souls, while the new Jalopy Race Track's first race just the Sunday before had attracted "a crowd estimated from two to three thousand." Conway formed and spearheaded the Orange County Anti-Racing Association and set as its goal the banning through legal means of Sunday racing. Their zeal was stymied, however, when the county attorney advised the board of commissioners that it had no legal right "to levy a license tax on [racing], nor could it limit or ban races without special legislation," and so the board took no action on the matter.

Meanwhile, the show must go on. The following Sunday, Mother's Day no less, Buck Baker beat Lee Petty, Fireball Roberts, and twenty-nine other drivers to win the one-hundred-mile Grand National late model race in a '56 Chrysler 300B before eight thousand cheering fans. His reward? Eleven hundred dollars. Only seventeen cars managed to finish the grueling race. The Reverends Conway and Reckard might have wagged their finger at the "one bad mishap. . . . Dick Beaty of Charlotte, in a '56 Ford, rolled his car. He was not seriously injured." And they could not have been happy with the article's closing statement: "Baker received a special trophy afterward from Miss Fay Collins, a pretty Hillsboro girl, plus a rewarding kiss."

HEADING back over toward the bleachers, Bill, Charlie, and I dodged briar bushes and potholes along the front stretch, then stepped into the treeline and climbed a clay bank. I still could not see anything resembling a grandstand. Then Bill knocked down a spiderweb as he parted the outstretched arms of two intertwined shrubs, and sprawling out before us were long rows of cracked concrete, slithering with vines and half-buried in dead leaves. This place was almost frightening, like one of those ancient, abandoned Buddhist temples built in the jungles of Thailand, where the humans have finally given up and Nature has returned to reclaim her own. I felt if I could only listen closely enough, I would hear the unstoppable roots of living, breathing plants driving their tentacles deep beneath the man-made structure to drink up every drop of moisture, rain, and dew, taking advantage of every crack and fissure, slowly squeezing the concrete into jagged clods, then crumbling them back into the very sand from which they were made. And if I listened more closely still, I might hear a more ancient sound, the wild, hollow drumming of hoofbeats as young braves raced one another along the packed clay of the Eno River, every bit as sacred to the Occoneechee tribe as the Ganges is to the Hindus.

My old friend John Blackfeather Jeffries, current chief of the Occoneechee tribe, told me once how when he was a child, he ran naked through this very forest, hunting deer with bow and arrow and fishing for bream and suckers with a hand-cut pole and twine. Smiling slyly, a twinkle shining in his dark eyes, he pointed off into the woods toward the raceway. "On summer Sundays, I'd sneak off from Mama and join up with my pals. We could hear the rumble like an earthquake down by the river. We didn't have no money to get in the track, so we'd climb them trees over on the backstretch and watch the race from up there. They called us the Tree People, black, white, and red, all poor folks, but we did have us some fun. Hell, we had the best seats in the house."

Now the only evidence that humans had ever been here at all was a few bent beer cans tossed among the weeds, no doubt left by the teenage daredevils on ATVs and dirt bikes that Bill had just recently convinced to take their hell-raising somewhere else. I fiddled with my camera and took photographs, knowing all the while that no picture could capture the sense of stilled reverence, the feeling of awe that comes when you see the slow but relentless power of the natural world in the face of humanity's puny attempts to take and keep a foothold. I turned back toward the track but saw only the barrier of trees. Yet I could still sense those ghost racers out there, flying nose to tail and balls to the wall, just beyond the green curtain.

I knew from the first moment that it was no accident we three had found ourselves together here on a warm summer morning. Like me, Bill has a theological background, and Charlie is on his own spiritual quest. We spoke of the quiet in what was once a very loud arena, of how it seemed we had moved back into the past as soon as we were swallowed by the trees, cocooned from our present lives. Our conversation moved on to the track restoration project, how it might be best to clear off and patch up a goodly stretch of the grandstands, along with a portion of the front stretch and the pit areas beyond, so that folks could see how the track might have looked when the concrete was new, even as they sat among the evidence of time's passing. "We could park a few old race cars out there on the track," said Bill. "That would do the trick."

We climbed the stands and threaded our way through the trees to what was once the front gate of the speedway, fallen aside now, only rusted sheets of corrugated metal folded over and hanging from fence wire.

The clapboard ticket office was all caved in, one corner still upright but leaned over to the side like a wounded soldier left standing after a pitched battle. Downhill a ways stood all that was left of the bathroom, a glorified outhouse. On the outside, in faded hand-painted letters, we could still read a message from a darker and more dangerous time: near one end of the building, "MEN" and at the far end, "NO NEGROES ALLOWED." We looked at one another in silence, shook our heads, and padded softly away along the carpet of pine needles.

BY March 1957 the North Orange Ministerial Association, formed in part to fight alongside Conway's anti-racing league, took their crusade to the state level, petitioning the North Carolina Legislature to preserve "the tradition of a peaceful and restful Sunday which has its roots in our spiritual heritage." Despite their efforts, including local minister Dr. Charles Maddry's portrayal of local racing as "endangering life" and a "desecration of the Sabbath," the county board remained unmoved.

Holding firm to their convictions, the ministers won a decisive battle by enlisting the aid of State Senator Edwin S. Lanier who, along with the help of Representative John W. Umstead, gained passage of a bill banning Sunday racing in Orange County by the state Committee on Cities, Counties, and Towns. In April the county board finally but reluctantly approved the measure, which also stipulated age limits for drivers (no one under eighteen) and forced track owners to obtain expensive casualty and liability insurance for both racers and spectators. Violators would be subject to fines or imprisonment.

Bill France, a savvy politician in his own right and, according to the *News*, "the automobile racing czar who has promoted his NASCAR sponsored tracks into a reported million dollar enterprise," went before the antiracing ministers to plead his case for a compromise that would postpone the institution of the ban and "limit the races to certain specific Sundays during the year." His words fell on deaf ears, however, as the ministers insisted that their primary motive was "preserving the sanctity of the Sabbath."

There is no public record, but one suspects at this point France must have done some behind-the-scenes lobbying, turning his considerable skills of persuasion on the members of the county board. Less than a month later, three of the four commissioners who had approved the antiracing bill flip-flopped, reversing that action in favor of France's proposed compromise. And what an ingenious proposal it was: to hear France tell it, he was willing to cut back his operation to stage only four races per year at each of the two tracks, but in reality he would salvage half the local racing season. His efforts turned out to be in vain. Within a week and despite the backsliding board of commissioners' recommendation in favor of France's compromise, the Sunday race-ban bill in its original form had passed the State Senate with almost no opposition and become law. The war between religion and racing was done, and the Christian soldiers had won.

Or so it seemed. As the man said, history ain't over yet. The popularity of stock car racing continued to spread like wildfire, and by 1961 France had announced plans for a new three-quarter-mile asphalt track complete with "all modern conveniences and a large concrete grandstand." What's more, just four years after losing the battle between Christian ministers and racing promoters, France's track was once again staging its races on Sunday.

This development was no doubt due as much to a lack of enforcement on the part of police as to any amendment in the law. After all, on the national scene, despite recent incidents like the failed Bay of Pigs invasion and the imminent standoff between President Kennedy and Russian Premier Khrushchev over the installation of nuclear weapons in Cuba, Senator McCarthy had been humbled by his own self-righteousness and the worst of the Red Scare was over. Perhaps America's postwar nerves had finally begun to settle down.

But one intriguing historical footnote might shed some light on this change in the attitude of the local authorities: That same year Bill France sold to the town of Hillsboro four acres of prime property, just down the Eno River from his speedway, for the construction of a sewage treatment plant. And wouldn't you know, for his efforts France received free water and sewage taps at the track.

It seems the devil's work is never done. Two years later, above an advertisement for Dewar's White Label Scotch Whiskey, the *News* ran an article accompanied by a large photograph showing a sultry, "leopard-skin coated" Jayne Mansfield riding around the Hillsboro speedway in the pace car and signing autographs for wide-eyed fans. The writer's closing words only served to confirm his righteous brethren's worst fears: "The crowd of 15,000 was estimated by racing officials to be split about evenly in attention to the visiting guest of honor in the judges' box and to the 150-mile Grand National Race."

At least in part because of the resistance of the local religious authorities, France finally gave up on Occoneechee Speedway. In 1968 he shut down the operation and moved his considerable resources to Alabama, where he had bought an eighteen-hundred-acre site forty miles east of Birmingham, not far from the Cosa River. There he built the biggest and fastest stock car track of them all: the Talladega Superspeedway, a 2.66-mile kidney-shaped and asphalt-coated giant where in the very next year the speeds and the crowds far outdistanced any ever reached at Occoneechee. In fact, you could fit the old Hillsboro track in the infield at Talladega with plenty of room to spare. I can't help but wonder if the city and county fathers back in North Carolina, once they saw the tremendous economic boon brought to central Alabama by the new state-of-the-art speedway, were ever sorry they took on Bill France. The protectors of morality and decency might well have won the battle, but at some level, it seems, they lost the war.

ON the way back to our vehicles, Bill talked of the sense of responsibility he feels toward this hallowed place, the need to take good care of an early relic of racing culture. He knows the latest battle for the soul of Occoneechee Speedway is far from over. Although the land was recently included in the National Register of Historic Places, thus protecting it from developers, the official Department of Transportation plan is still to run the bypass over the grandstands, across the front stretch, and then over the third turn of the track. Nevertheless Bill and the trustees of Ayr Mount are doing all they can to preserve the past in the face of an uncertain future.

As I drove across the interstate overpass toward home, it came to me that the NASCAR dynasty built by Big Bill France might well learn a lesson here. As multimillionaires build newer and faster speedways to take advantage of huge metropolitan markets, smaller tracks like the one at North Wilkesboro, North Carolina—now a ghost track on its way to slipping back into the earth like the Occoneechee Speedway—are being left quite literally in the dust. Yet it was on the shoulders of short tracks like these that NASCAR was built, and the France family, which still owns and runs the old man's racing empire, seems hell-bent on letting go its roots in pursuit of the Almighty Dollar. Granted, several of the current tracks boast buildings full of old race cars and other memorabilia, but why not invest in living museums set down on the very land where those pioneers first strapped on their helmets and fired up their engines? The tourist dollars alone would pay the bills, and we would all be the richer for it.

Turning onto New Hope Road and heading out into the country, I pushed my old Ford truck a little faster in the slightly banked curves and gunned its new V-8 down a flat, open stretch. The engine rumbled beneath me, its heartbeat fast and steady. The warm wind whipped through my hair, and I smiled to think of the very last Grand National race at Occoneechee Speedway, one of those rare moments in history when you can see the torch being passed to a new generation. It was September 1968. That old charger Lee Petty had taken the checkered flag at one of the first Hillsboro races back in 1950, but this day it was his son who won in an electric blue Plymouth, outlasting David Pearson and finishing seven laps ahead of the field. As fate would have it, Richard Petty went on to become the winningest driver in NASCAR history. Call me sentimental, but I feel a fierce pride knowing the King of Stock Car Racing got his start right here in my own backyard.

CHAPTER THREE

So What's the Point?

'm an evangelist for NASCAR. I spread the gospel of racing every chance I get. Oftentimes I find myself preaching to the choir, those who are already converted, who understand the joy and excitement that come with a firsthand experience of the power and the glory that is stock car racing. Other times I speak to the unenlightened, whose eyes and ears have not yet been opened. Because I have spent many long years as a graduate student, worked as an administrative assistant at one university, and teach at another, I rub elbows with a lot of very intelligent folks who have yet to see the light. Do not mistake me for one who is anti-intellectual. Mistrust of education is one of the worst errors committed by far too many evangelicals. Nonetheless, even the highly educated suffer their various ignorances, and liberals who refuse to openly consider any way other than their own are as blind as any fundamentalist. It was Jesus who asked, "Can the blind lead the blind? Shall they not both fall into the ditch?" (Luke 6:39). Although racing's audience is growing by leaps and bounds, spreading, it would seem, to the four corners of the Earth, there are still pockets of darkness where benighted souls toil away in disregard. The ivory tower is one such enclave, so my missionary work is cut out for me. Hence this book.

Most intellectuals have a hard time seeing the charm of racing. Over the past few years, a typical conversation with one of my academic colleagues has run like this: I'm talking with a professor in the lounge of the Department of Philosophy at Duke University. "Why would you waste a perfectly good Sunday afternoon," he asks, "watching forty-odd rednecks drive around in circles?"

Heresy, eh? No, an opportunity! I answer right back, "Those are forty of the world's most talented drivers, some of the best athletes around, and besides, they're not all rednecks. A couple of the drivers are even from California."

"But whoever they are," he replies, "at the end of the day all they have done is drive a car. Anyone can do that."

"Yes, anyone can drive a car, but they can't drive five hundred miles at almost 200 miles per hour mere inches from forty other cars going just as fast."

He smiles. "Sorry, L. D., I just do not see how you can call automobile racing a sport."

"Okay," I say, taking up the challenge, "let me ask you this. How can you sit for four hours on a Sunday afternoon and watch grown men use very thin sticks to smack tiny little balls at a very small hole in the ground a long way off? Besides," I add with a wink, "some of these men wear *knickers*, for crying out loud!"

"But have you ever played golf?" he asks, his eyes widening a bit. "It's an extremely difficult game."

"I've played enough to know it's beyond difficult. Golf is downright tragic."

"But that is precisely the appeal," he says. "Of all the men and women who play golf, how many can finish eighteen holes in under seventy strokes, week in and week out? I submit that those who can do so earn their paychecks, due to the very difficulty of what they manage to accomplish."

"All right, of all the men and women who drive cars, how many could control a three-thousand-pound, eight-hundred-horsepower fire-breathing dragon, pass the competition in a thirty-three-degree banked turn, dodge a wreck at 150-plus miles an hour, all while strapped into a sheet-metal-skinned steel cage where temperatures in summertime can reach 150 degrees? Talk about earning your paycheck."

"But that is not sport," he says, fingering the cover of the *Journal of Philosophy* on the table between us. "That is insanity."

"Yes, drivers do get killed from time to time. Dale Earnhardt might've been the most famous racer to die, but he's by no means the only one. To me the miracle of stock car racing is that so many drivers arrive home safely every week. And you can smirk if you want, but the danger is part of the appeal. Millions of television viewers don't watch 'America's Scariest Police Chases' for nothing."

"That does not speak well for the intelligence level of the racing audience."

Stealing a line from my brother and struggling to keep the anger out of my voice, I say, "Sorry, man, but

I resent that remark. You can make this about class or educational level if you want to, but there's no denying the widespread draw of racing. Hell, these days there are as many Mercedes and BMWs in the racetrack parking lots as there are pickup trucks."

"Nevertheless, no matter who invests their capital in the business of racing, it is not a sport."

I change my tack. "You're right. It's not a sport—it's a *religion*."

"Come again?"

"Racing is a religion, a cult of true believers with their own rituals, myths, and a system of ethics that rival Confucianism."

He says with a wave of his hand, "That is patently absurd." But I can tell by his tone that he's curious.

"I'm guessing you've never been to a race."

"I have watched the Indianapolis 500 on television."

"Different racers, same deal. Let's start with the obvious. There are specifically religious rituals as part of every race. For one thing, a vast multitude of people stand and bow their heads together as a chaplain or local minister prays for the sportsmanship and safety of all involved."

"Yes," he says, "but the same practice occurs before many baseball games."

"True, but that's a cult of a different color. You're only proving my point. Then there are patriotic rituals, the singing of the National Anthem and plenty of flag-waving."

"So you're talking about civil religion—"

"Exactly. All these people who've come together for fun pause for a moment to recognize a greater power, whether it be God or nation. What's the difference between such public rituals and folks gathering in a church or temple or mosque to offer their time and money and energy to a higher calling?"

"So there are certain religious aspects to racing. That does not, however, make it a religion."

"Well, then, while you were watching the Indy 500, did you notice how every aspect of the race is governed by strict rules and regulations, right down to one one-hundredth of an inch measurements in the engine and suspension of the race cars? The NASCAR rule book reads like the book of Deuteronomy! All those picky rules Moses brought down from the mountaintop—"

"But," he insists, "those were religious laws, rules governing the ethical conduct of God's people."

"Precisely. Racing has its ethics, not unlike the Roman Catholic Church. There are official, written regulations, the racing rule book—racing's Bible, you might call it—passed down from the higher-ups. These regulations govern the public behavior of all the drivers and their teams as well as the car owners. If you break the Church's commandments, you do penance to atone for your wrongs. If you disobey racing's rules, it'll cost you a fine or even suspension, a temporary excommunication. And then there are the unwritten rules every driver knows. To disobey them is to risk damnation in the eyes of your competition."

"What do you mean 'damnation'?" he asks. "Can you illustrate your point?"

"Sure. A few years back, Earnhardt was chasing the race leader, Terry Labonte, in the last laps at Bristol, NASCAR's shortest track where it's almost impossible to pass. At the end of a Bristol race, very few cars have all four fenders, and none gets back to the garage without streaks of paint from a half-dozen other vehicles. One of the unwritten rules of racing is that you can tap someone in front of you to move them out of your way, but you can't cause them to spin out. It's a rule Earnhardt was infamous for stretching to its absolute limit—that's one reason everybody called him the Intimidator. So this time he managed to get his front end to the inside of Labonte's rear fender, but Earnhardt bumped the other car so hard Labonte spun out. Everybody knew Earnhardt had stepped over the line, even Earnhardt. You should've seen his Cheshire Cat smile during the postrace interview in the winner's circle. That was the closest I ever saw him come to an apology."

I can tell by his puzzled look that the details are lost on my philosopher friend, but he doesn't let it go. "So I suppose you are going to argue that the crowds of spectators are the congregation in this religion of racing."

"Exactly. The fans are the faithful few, the righteous remnant saved from the boredom of their everyday lives by the mystical religious experience of raw power and awesome speed. The fans I know live out their fantasies at the racetrack. That's why they bond with a particular driver, just like many youngsters want to be like Michael

Jordan or Tiger Woods. It's all about being lifted up out of our all-too-ordinary lives and feeling that, even if only for a few moments, we could walk on water, or hit the thirty-foot jumper at the buzzer, or smack a tee shot three hundred yards, chip to the green, and sink the twelve-foot putt. To put it in more philosophical terms, it's all about transcendence."

"Nonetheless," he says, "racing may or may not be a religion, it may or may not be sport, but it is most assuredly uninteresting to watch."

"I'm guessing that's because you've never seen a race live and in person. Hey, don't knock it 'til you've tried it. There's just nothing like being there for intensity. Think Ben Hur and the chariot races—it's one hell of a spectacle. No other sport, if you will grant me that term for the moment, can touch it for sheer excitement."

"Forty-odd cars driving in circles."

"Yes, forty-odd monstrous machines running hell-bent for leather, faster than God ever intended humans to go." I can feel the evangelistic fire in my bones as I lean forward and wave my hands across the tabletop. "When that green flag drops and the pack busts loose, the first time they come by you, every ounce of oxygen is sucked out of the air. There's nothing you can do but hold your breath, scream if you can, and pray your heart doesn't stop. All your worries, all your cares, tomorrow, and yesterday drop away, and you're caught up in the present moment, what one theologian called the Eternal Now. Nothing else matters. And if that ain't religion, I don't know what is. Like Christians slain in the Spirit,

Buddhists rapt in meditation, you are taken beyond words, beyond even thought, transported to a place of pure feeling. What was that little hand-scribbled note they found in the pocket of your French philosopher, Pascal? *'Joy! Joy! Joy!'* "

"But L. D., I was not exposed to such things in my youth. I come from a different cultural background, the gentlemanly sports."

"Football is gentlemanly? Basketball a noncontact sport? Hell, even John Daly, golf's bad boy, has had his drunken brawl. And as for tennis, one name: John McEnroe. "Okay, let me ask you this, Doc: do you like to drive?"

"Yes, I enjoy the experience of traveling in an expertly designed, precisely tuned vehicle."

"Then you're halfway there."

"Yet the Indy cars travel at much faster speeds."

"No wonder you don't care for racing. Those aren't cars. They're hot dog weenies with wheels. They look nothing like the BMW you drive. At least stock car fans enjoy the illusion of watching their own Taurus or Monte Carlo or Charger out there on the track."

"European automotive technology is far superior to anything made in America."

"Maybe so, but then stock car fans practice that patriotic civil religion of 'one nation under God.' "

"Perhaps Marx was right," he said with a glint in his eye. "Racing, like religion, is the opiate of the people."

"Here's another question: when you first got your driver's license, how long was it before you floored the accelerator in your dad's car just to see how fast it would go?"

He smiled.

"*That's* the need for speed," I said, "the primal human urge to go as fast as possible, and even faster. It's the very thing that drives the space race, what took Wilbur and Orville down to Kill Devil Hills, the very force that pushed some foolhardy early human to risk life and limb by climbing on the back of an unsuspecting wild horse. We all feel this urge from the time we first learn to walk. It's not enough for a toddler to waddle from here to there. Why walk when you can run? Tricycles and bicycles, roller skates and surfboards, motorbikes and go-karts, we all want to go fast, and some of us want to go fastest. Even Henry Ford started out as a racer."

"Well," he said, checking his watch and standing to go, "you have given me much to contemplate."

"Don't just think about it. Do something. Here's the deal: the local boys will be running over at Orange County Speedway this Saturday night. The cars can't fly nearly as fast as the archangels of NASCAR, but the fans are friendly, the beer is cold, and they serve a mean fried boloney sandwich. Best of all, you can get closer to the action than you ever could at Daytona or Darlington. Are you game?"

"I suppose it would be a good opportunity to study a different subculture of American society. But I will pass on the baloney sandwich, thank you."

Sadly, such conversations have produced few converts. For all their openmindedness, academics are a tough crowd. I suspect this has as much to do with socio-economic class as it does with preference in pastimes.

Recently I was invited to present my research on religion and racing to a gathering of historians from local universities. The invitation is a sign not only of racing's increasing popularity but also of a shift within higher education itself. There was a time not that very long ago when few if any respectable scholars would stoop to studying matters related to popular culture, unless of course such studies were limited to the lifestyles of the lower classes in ancient Greece or the underlings in the plays of Shakespeare. Increasingly, however, "how the other half lives" has become fair game. Almost every institute of higher education can boast specialists in pop culture, experts in everything from the subcultures of rock 'n' roll music to changing trends in the tastes of television viewers to the cultural implications of popular fashion in clothing. The course I teach on religion and racing would have been all but inconceivable only a few decades ago.

The historians I spoke to seemed both interested in the history of stock car racing and quite perplexed by the widespread attention the sport currently commands. Their questions and comments were for the most part insightful, but very soon into our discussion I couldn't help but notice an odd quirk in the behavior of several who were gathered around the table. Almost without fail, whenever a question or comment betrayed some prior knowledge of NASCAR in particular or racing in general, the speaker felt it necessary to distance him or herself from that knowledge with a smirk, a giggle, or an offhand remark about how little they *really* know about the sport.

Maybe I have a chip on my shoulder, but it did not help matters that many of these historians spoke with either a distinctly non-Southern accent, the polished and polysyllabic smoothness of those who have spent much of their lives in libraries, or both. The meeting went on this way for some time, until I finally felt the need to interrupt the conversation, risk committing the social sin of bad manners, and ask outright if there is some unspoken rule that any serious thinker should be embarrassed to betray before their colleagues the possibility that such lowbrow goings-on might actually be worthy of attention. There was a moment of stunned silence until one of the assembled group spoke up to give what church folks call a personal testimony to her longtime love of racing and an ongoing pride in its accomplishments. The rest of the meeting was polite. If I had embarrassed any or all or only myself, my colleagues were gracious and seemed genuinely grateful. Missionary work is not always easy, and often not very pretty.

And so, like any good evangelist, I turn the message directly to you: if you wonder why auto racing is the fastest-growing spectator sport in America, why not find the nearest small-time racetrack like the Orange County Speedway, off US 501 thirty minutes north of Durham, North Carolina? Here every other weekend from late spring through early fall, local daredevils race—before enthusiastic crowds for prize money and a fierce brand of glory—headlong around a three-eighths-of-a-mile asphalt track. On my first Saturday night at the track, Raleigh's own Deac McCaskill, a nineteen-year-old prodigy who won his first race when he was only thirteen, took the checkered flag in both seventy-five-lap feature races. Almost every inch of the way, McCaskill dueled bumper to bumper and wheel to wheel with the tiny town of Bahama's favorite son Scott Riggs, who has since made his way up through the NASCAR ranks and now runs in the Nextel Cup Series. Both drivers managed to avoid several accidents that left more than one car with fewer than four fenders.

During the second race, when a caravan of cars bunched up in the "corner" coming out of turn four, the Chevy Monte Carlo driven by Timmy Miller of Raleigh was forced up against the wall. Somehow he ended up sliding on his reinforced top the length of the front stretch across the start/finish line before lightly tapping the wall in the first turn. Miller had unstrapped himself and climbed out of the overturned vehicle before the thin trail of gasoline strewn along the straightaway had burned itself out. Track officials go to great lengths to ensure that such mishaps occur as seldom as possible, but I suspect the crowd roared its appreciation both for the crash and sparks of the wreck as well as for Miller escaping relatively unscathed.

Race drivers risk injury not unlike athletes in other sports—for example, "giving up the body" to drive the basketball down the lane or take the football up the middle or push the puck to the net. Yet racing balls to the wall in a reinforced steel cage on wheels alongside fifteen others for 150 or more laps hazards more than a concussion or a torn anterior cruciate ligament. A driver stares Death in the eye and not just for an instant, as any of us might in our better moments, but for a solid hour, a feat that requires not only a space-walking astronaut's self-control but also a galvanized trust among drivers who are sworn to outwit and outrun each other any way they can, yet whose severest censure—fistfight, anyone?—is evoked when one driver endangers the life of another. Due to the proximity of calamity and death, a local preacher begins each race with a prayer for the safety of everyone involved.

To get some idea of what short-track racing is all about, imagine taking a jaunt up the Jersey Turnpike from Philly to Newark at ninety-plus-miles-per-hour in a pack of fifteen other vehicles. Okay, maybe you've already had this experience; perhaps you make a similar commute on a daily basis. If you have never driven fast nor felt the desire to do so, you may not appreciate a thing I've said, but one thing you will notice at any speedway these days is that racing is not a hobby followed only by gearheads. In fact, many such smaller tracks provide a family section where alcoholic beverages and the rowdy behavior that all too often come along with them are not allowed.

As with any form of competition, be it soccer or golf or even poker, if you watch racing closely and listen to the fans, you begin to notice many levels of strategy. For instance, there is the art and craft of drafting, which works according to the principle that an object traveling in the slipstream of another object just ahead will move more quickly using less energy than an object having to split the air on its own; hence the long lines of aerodynamically designed cars racing only inches apart at literally breakneck speeds. You might notice this phenomenon if you're crazy enough to follow closely behind an eighteen-wheeler on the interstate. Then there are those beehives of activity just inside the asphalt oval of the racetrack known as the pits, a glorified gas station where racers get a new set of tires, a tankful of gas, and the windshield washed not in an afternoon, not even in an hour, but within the space of thirty seconds, and where a mechanic's split-second hesitation means a driver can lose a lap or more to competitors moving at almost one hundred miles per hour out on the track.

What's more, the race at a track like Orange County Speedway is to the Daytona 500 what a minor league baseball game at the local ballpark is to an Atlanta Braves or New York Yankees game in the big league. That is, for a fraction of the ticket cost, you can see the action up close and personal, and a hot dog and soda won't cost you an arm and a leg. Trackside, just like at a rock concert if you stand close enough to the stage, the appeal is visceral: you are literally swallowed up in sound. You do not so much hear the noise of the fire-breathing dragons circling past you as you feel it in your bones and sinews, as if your entire body were a vibrating eardrum. Imagine sitting face-to-face with an hour-long earthquake, or eating popcorn on the lip of an erupting volcano. Needless to say, a pair of earplugs is standard equipment for any race fan.

FOR many but certainly not all, their initial experience at the track is an unforgettable one. How my mom's daddy managed to pull off the blasphemy of taking me to my first stock car race is still a mystery. I was working on my fourth year of not missing a single week of Sunday school and had the faux-gold one-year pin on my Sunday dress shirt, along with a medallion dangling underneath for each additional year, to prove it. Mom had me on a righteous roll, but somehow Papa hornswoggled her into letting me skip church to go with him to the racetrack one sunny Sunday morning in the summer of 1964.

Whenever I drive out to the speedway, I get to feeling like I am eight years old again, sitting next to Papa on the wide front seat of his '63 Impala winding our way up Highway 221 to a little half-mile asphalt oval in Harris, North Carolina. A filterless Camel dangling from his stubbled lip and a Pabst Blue Ribbon balanced between his legs, Papa drove full throttle, his wiry mechanic's fingers twisting the radio knob like he was tightening a radiator cap. When the nasal twang of Lefty Frizzell's "Saginaw, Michigan" rose up through the static, Papa started talking again about what a hellbender his favorite racer, Fireball Roberts, had been. As if to fulfill the prophecy of his nickname, Papa's tragic hero had burned to death just weeks before in a bone-crunching crash at Charlotte Motor Speedway. I had never seen Papa cry, so I looked out my window at the green paradise of the Carolina foothills rolling by while he got all choked up and tears rolled down his wrinkly face. Once he simmered down, I patted his arm and told him I was pretty sure Mr. Fireball was up in Heaven with Jesus now. He flicked the flaring butt of his cigarette out the window and tugged a handkerchief from the big back pocket of his coveralls to honk his nose in it.

These days I miss Papa something awful—those godforsaken Camels and an otherwise less than healthy lifestyle finally did him in—but along the smooth curves of US 501 on the way out to Orange County Speedway I often feel his presence with me as real as the red-tailed hawks circling over my truck. He taught me to love the noise and speed of racing and the daredevil spirit that drives men (and the occasional woman) to put life and limb on the line for a few bucks and an outside shot at fame and fortune.

Forgive my evangelistic fervor, but if for whatever reason you just don't get the appeal of stock car racing and you're understandably unwilling to risk a hundred bucks a pop for tickets to find out what all the buzz is about, please allow me to close this sermon by extending a call to you and yours: why not pack up the kids, pick up some earplugs, and head out to the track this weekend to witness the competition up close? The drinks are cold, the food is down-home good, and tickets cost only a fraction of what you'd spend at Daytona or Darlington. Kids usually get in free, and the best thing of all? Since races are run on Saturday nights, they won't even have to miss Sunday school.

CHAPTER FOUR

Racing for Whitenecks

If you're still a doubter as to the spiritual aspect at the very heart of racing—its depth dimension, to borrow Paul Tillich's term—perhaps you aren't paying enough attention to the vehicle that cradles and carries you from place to place every day. In this day of suburban living and long commutes, many of us spend as much time on the road as we do in the bosom of our families. We eat in our cars, sometimes nap there, relax to our favorite tunes, even shave or put on makeup. For some, these machines take on their own personalities. We even give them names, for crying out loud! Like an old song can take us back to another time and place, most of us remember the very first car we owned—the pride, excitement, and freedom we felt to have our own wheels.

Well, you might call me a redneck, a romantic, or a misguided fool, but I'm a sucker for old trucks. Twenty years ago, part of my personal therapy as a recovering fundamentalist was to shell out five hundred hard-earned dollars for a yellow 1957 Chevrolet pickup truck, which looked like someone had chopped the classic '57 sedan in half and put an open, and very rusty, box on the back. I had been wandering in something of an adolescent nightmare for a few years before, denying myself the pleasures of this world in hopes of a better one to come. Getting my hands on such a vital chunk of growling, steaming steel helped to put my feet back on the ground. The first time I climbed up under the front end to check an oil leak, I almost wept with nostalgia. The years and miles of accumulated grease and grime coating the undercarriage like primeval muck smelled just like the coveralls my mom's daddy worked in.

For as long as I knew him, Papa was a grease monkey, fixing people's cars for a living. Whenever I saw him leaving for Blackwood's Garage in the morning, his coveralls were smooth and white as mountain snow, but when he returned home in the evening, they were wrinkled and dirty from head to foot, smeared with every shade and thickness of grease, oil, and grime. This rich automotive stew gives off a very distinctive bouquet, so I christened the truck Prince Albert, after the tobacco Papa smoked and in honor of the man who taught me the physical joy of hunkering down on the fender of a wounded vehicle and leaning under the hood to turn a greasy wrench and cuss a stubborn bolt.

The therapy must have worked, because I recovered enough from the ascetic dreamscape of seminary to return to graduate school in 1986. Unfortunately, as a student I could no longer afford to keep up the maintenance on Albert, and it was a sin to watch the old soldier go downhill. Rather than put him out to pasture, I sold him to a neighbor for twice what I had originally paid. Before he took Albert away, I told the guy, "When you get him fixed up all nice and pretty, don't even drive by my house. It'll only hurt my feelings!"

I used the money to buy my first motorcycle for the commute to Wake Forest University. The two-wheeler was a lot of fun despite (and partly because of) the dangers, but man, did I miss having a truck! For one thing, people will flat run over you on a bike, but no sedan-driving, cell phone–talking type A will dare to challenge two tons of solid American steel. For another, most folks don't often need a truck to haul things, but when they do, a fire-breathing V-8 up front and a four-by-six-foot bed in back sure do come in handy. Finally, if the truck is an elder statesman like Albert, you don't even need to worry about those inevitable dings, nicks, and scratches that automotive metal is heir to. Like the wrinkles in Papa's dear face, the scars just give the old boy character.

So I went several years without a truck, until my dad cut me a good deal on his 1984 Nissan, a peppy little four-cylinder with a steering wheel about as big around and tight as Jack's hatband. These were strange days. I had moved to Chapel Hill, where grad school ground me up and spit me out, and then I floundered for a while, working part-time here and there, unsure of who I was. Misty, the name Dad's wife gave the truck, served me well, but she never really felt mine. It was plain to see I had never committed to the relationship because my heart knocked like a blown engine whenever I saw a

'66 Chevy shortbed or, the absolute ultimate in pickups, a fat-fendered, friendly faced '56 Ford, the truck I had originally hunted before running across the '57 Chevy.

Then God intervened, or at least an act of God, to use the insurance company's term. I went out one morning after a nasty windstorm to find that a tree limb weighing almost half as much as the Nissan had scored a direct hit on poor Misty. The formerly flat top of her cab was now V-shaped and her hood smashed like Muhammad Ali's jaw. One look and the insurance man decided she was totaled, so I arm wrestled him out of enough money to buy the 1966 Ford F-100 I drive today.

Of course, I had gone looking for a mid-'60s Chevy, but every one I found was either too far gone or far too dear. Then one fateful day I drove over to Kernersville to check out a Ford pickup listed in a local trade paper. As soon as I laid eyes on Perry, the salt-of-the-earth auto mechanic who owned the truck, his blue uniform neatly cleaned and starched, his hair and beard trimmed and combed, I knew he was the kind of guy, like Papa, who would take pains to tighten down every screw and bolt.

In the ten years or so I've owned Ol' Blue, I've come a long way toward finding myself. Except for occasional relapses of self-righteousness, I've pretty much exorcised my fundamentalist demons. What's more, I hardly ever get that grad school twitch in my eye when some poor fool references Jacques Derrida. I've been around long enough to know that just because something is flashy and new doesn't necessarily make it good or long-lasting. And even though we should accept and appreciate what is bequeathed to us from our forebears, some-how we still have to make this world our own.

How can an inanimate object take on something of the features of our life and speak to us, as well as to others, of who we are? I can't say exactly, but I do know Ol' Blue has been a faithful friend. To my eyes he's a hand-some devil, with the smooth classic lines of Detroit's finest year: think of the '66 Ford Galaxie, the Chevy Impala, and the Mustang fastback. He stands tall, so I ride above the swirl of traffic like Rowdy Yates on a cattle drive. His faded paint is as soft to the eye as my baby-blue suede shoes, and like a good old pair of blue jeans, he gets a little lighter, a bit more comfortable with every wash. He is a tad drafty in the winter, but his 2/60 air conditioning (two windows down at sixty miles per hour) keeps me nice and cool all summer, that is, as long as I keep rollin', rollin', rollin'.

I must confess, like even the best of friends, Ol' Blue leaves me in the lurch from time to time. I forgive his occasional refusal to roll out of bed in the morning be-cause he just turned over 350,000 miles, which must be about ninety-five in human years, and Lord knows, the older we get the more maintenance we require. Never-theless, his eight-cylindered heart still beats stronger than mine and never skips a beat. As Hazel Motes says in the novel *Wise Blood*, "A lightnin' bolt couldn't stop it." I think to myself whenever I feel that sweet little tremble all through the chassis each time the crankshaft turns, *As long as it quivers, he's alive.* Even if he burns a little oil or fouls a plug now and then, he packs twice the acceleration of many young whippersnappers half his age. The bottom line is this: as long as I pamper him, he always comes through for me in the clutch. I like to think Ol' Blue's a pickup truck my granddaddy would be proud to turn a wrench on.

Many fans love racing because they care about cars, their own in particular and even more so the ones that run loud and fast. A crucial challenge in any attempt to understand, much less explain, such affection of humans for machines is the very fact that this relationship seems to run deeper in human experience than rational argument is able to go. It is, in a word—and a fancy one at that—ineffable, which is to say we are confronted with a truth that simply cannot be expressed in words. (Ain't it just like English to have a word for that which cannot be told in human language?) More than once while writing the book you now hold, I have been sorely tempted to throw up my hands, shut down the computer, and yell, "I give up! Who feels it knows it, and *that's that*."

Yet such a surrender would be not only irresponsible but also, I believe, unnecessary. I say this in part because I happened to have grown up in the South. As frustrating as it may be to Yankees, when Southerners cannot explain in a straightforward manner something we know to be true, what we do is a tell a story, a tale that may guide the listener through the process by which we ourselves have come to know this truth. In this respect, one thinks of Jesus' parables and the Jataka tales of the Buddha. Just because we cannot explain a certainty does not mean we cannot illustrate its veracity. Hence the approach I have so often taken in my argument is not so much objective as it is narrative and at times anecdotal. And so, as a way to show that to which words just won't do justice, let me share a story. Truth be known, my favorite form of racing is not the round-and-round of oval tracks but the side-by-side straight lines of a drag race, where missile-shaped Top Fuel dragsters and funny cars that are anything but stock cover a quarter-mile in less than five seconds at speeds approaching 325 miles an hour. And so it was that on a Saturday morning maybe ten years ago, my older brother Frank and I loaded my pickup truck with firewood, sleeping bags, and a bag of chocolate candy and drove out of the Piedmont into the coastal plain flatlands down east to the Rockingham Dragway for the Winston Select Invitational Drag Racing Championships. If the first thing that pops into your head upon reading that statement is "redneck" or "Bubba" or "cross-dressing," then read on.

This would be the first time I ever spent the weekend at the drag races sober, in deference to Frank, who had been on the wagon for a decade, as well as to my younger brother James, who was driving up from Myrtle Beach with his seven-year-old son Jimi Dean and who had also been sober since an automobile accident the December before we gathered at the races. But if we weren't planning to drink and smoke and snort ourselves into oblivion, why on Earth did we go? We went to the Rock, as we affectionately call the concrete and asphalt dragway, seeking the mystical experience of transcendence, to climb out of the tedious boredom of our everyday existence and taste the sweet nectar of life.

I know this sounds highfalutin for a couple of Virginia-born, South Carolina–reared good ol' boys who, like so many of our Yankee brethren and sistren, have settled for one reason or another here in the Old North State, but let me unpack it a little. My brothers and I met at the drag strip for the same reason that we like to ride motorcycles, in spite of the grief and anxious looks our family and friends and even total strangers give us about doing so: we wanted to look Death right in his bloodshot eye and stare until the Old Bastard blinked. I am not joking. Every time I ride my Honda Shadow, I imagine the Grim Reaper sitting on the seat behind me with his bony hands clutching my shoulders, and the day I cease sensing him there is the day I will no longer ride, because it is the constant threat of danger and death, which we tend to forget when entombed, if you will, in a car, that keeps me honest—and scared safe.

But watching these men and women defy death in their hot rods was not the only reason we went to Rockingham. We paid good money to see them risk their lives because they are a rare breed of scientist, their noisy experiments designed to push the envelope of speed and torque and human reflexes with all the precision and caution that automotive technology can muster. Like these brave souls we went to flirt with the danger, smell its fumes, feel its thunderous shudder.

And so we yelled at the tops of our lungs and tried not to blink whenever two dragsters tore past us side by side down the length of the quarter-mile track faster than you can say "internal combustion engine." Frank and I ran down the concrete bleachers to stand as near to the action as the guards would let us. Our shirts were all but whipped off by the windstorm swept up by machines too loud to hear; we could only feel them, our entire bodies become eardrums pounded by the controlled explosions of the engines.

We were caught up in the joyous, awe-filled gasp of the crowd when a long Top Fuel rail dragster, a sheet metal and iron missile laid over and set on wheels with a human strapped inside, careened out of control and flipped over, crossing the finish line rear end first at nearly three hundred miles per hour only five seconds after it left the starting line. Moments later, the driver climbed out and walked away waving his arms to let everyone know he lived to race again. I heard myself shouting between windstorms, "If they had wings, they'd fly!" During a break in the action, James, who before his wreck could have lifted Frank and me both with his bare hands, put his arms around our shoulders so we could help him climb slowly back up the bleachers to our seats.

On Saturday night, those revelers who could not afford a hotel room or who had simply chosen to camp out stood around their fires drinking, cursing, and howling down the moon. Many of them no doubt had worked several months or more to save enough money for the privilege of sleeping in their cars or in sleeping bags or blankets on the ground in the huge sandy parking lot dotted with pine trees and small spiny cactuses. Others, I suppose, were spending all or most of the past week's paycheck.

Dancing around our own campfire, Jimi Dean twirled sparklers, and Frank and James and I shot off the bottle rockets I had bought south of the state border and squirreled away after they were deemed illegal here in North Carolina. Somebody down deeper in the woods answered our volleys by firing off a few rounds with what must surely have been a high-caliber revolver. The more inebriated or at least less inhibited of our neighbors howled again and again far into the night, long after we had crawled into our tents to try to sleep. At times their keening formed a chorus so widespread and thick it seemed we were lost in the depths of the American wilderness, surrounded by a ravenous pack of werewolves.

"Listen to those mindless yahoos," Frank mumbled from his sleeping bag. "Like a bunch of dumb animals." *No,* I thought in the flickering light of the fire, these men and women never sat in a university chair much less endowed one, and will never own a business though they work to build them for others, but they are carving their names ever so briefly on the wet night air for the same reasons that the wealthy and powerful commemorate themselves with monuments, from pyramids to cathedrals to Trump Tower: to assure themselves that they live a life of consequence here on this Earth that not even Death itself can destroy.

MOST of the racing crowd had shelled out twenty-five dollars on Saturday and another thirty dollars on Sunday for access to the cheap seats lining one entire side of the track from starting line to finish, where mostly blue-collar blacks and whites and a handful of Native Americans rubbed elbows, not always amiably. There was the shirtless, monosyllabic white man who all day Saturday bought and drank his limit of two Budweisers at a time and grudgingly tolerated the four black men sitting next to us. His only interchange with them was a grunted request for one of the men, who wore a black baseball cap with Malcolm's X on it, to move his camera so he would not step on it. Several black youths sported T-shirts with the slogan "It's a black thing—you wouldn't understand." A white man wore a T-shirt with the crossed stars of the Confederate flag emblazoned across its front, captioned with "You wear your X, I'll wear mine." During a break in the action, Frank and I laughed nervously when we saw a bumper sticker on a truck in the parking lot which read, "Don't blame me. I voted for Jeff Davis."

But the most glaring example of discrimination during the weekend was not so much racial as economic— and much closer if not more damaging to the heartbeat of modern America. Ten dollars extra bought us a Pit Pass and access through a guarded gate to the other side of the track, where crewmen turned long wrenches on the beefed-up engines of funny cars, their entire sheet metal bodies lifted off and set aside to reveal their skeletal roll cages, electric chair seats, and the shining chrome and iron guts of the racing machines. Around the pit area nubile young women, grinning and friendly like the nymphs in beer commercials, wearing short shorts and tight T-shirts sporting the logos of cigarette manufacturers, walked up and asked us to fill out surveys for a giveaway of cigarettes, T-shirts, and more.

On this pricier side of the track the cultural mix shifted markedly toward the white middle class. The restrooms were less crowded here, and beneath the grandstands I found the coolest spot of the weekend. Like some fringe benefit for those who could afford a Pit Pass, there was even a light breeze blowing, carrying the unmistakably American smell of hot dog chili. No bean sprouts here, though unlike in years past bottled water was available alongside beer and cola.

Walking back to the campsite, James and I stepped around a man in his twenties limping along with a cane, his withered right arm hanging by his side. "Stroke?" I asked James when we were out of earshot. "Car wreck," he said and looked away. I shuddered to think of that cold starry night when James's car slipped into a roadside ditch before slamming the end of a concrete drainage pipe at fifty miles per hour. He came awfully close to dying. His only good fortune was to have dozed off and lost control directly across the road from a volunteer fire department, so that EMTs were with him only moments after they heard the collision. The last time Frank and I had traveled together to see him, he was in intensive care, his black-and-blue face swollen to twice its normal size and his shattered right leg strapped to a traction bar. This night as we sat amid our tents and drank Cokes and gnawed the good Colonel's fried chicken, James showed us the most recent X-rays. He held them up and let us look at them one after another against the light of the fire, until I could no longer see for the tears in my eyes. The eerie negative of one X-ray exposed the jagged edges where the large bone of his right leg had snapped in the middle and was patched together now by three ghastly white one-inch screws. The smaller leg bone had broken off at both ends and hung there suspended in meat, connected to the larger bone only by thin, dark bridges of calcium deposit. His hip was cracked and remained out of kilter because the break was found too late to correct without ruining the setting of the larger leg bone. But it was the X-ray of his right foot that pushed me to open weeping, for what had been the carefully fitted mosaic of delicate bones at the base of four of the five toes was now splintered as though he had set off a shoe bomb. "My God," I whispered to myself, "you *walk* on that!"

So, if the risk of speed is injuries like James's and the scars he will carry to his grave, then why the increasing popularity of racing sports? Why our recent cultural obsession with the extreme, whether in biking, skiing, climbing, or whatever? Why do otherwise perfectly sane, successful young people dive off bridges with a rubber band strapped to their ankles rather than go for leisurely rides through the countryside? Kurt Cobain is certainly not the first to have expressed and then acted out this generation's epigram, if not its epitaph: Boredom is the worst enemy. The lament over lethargy has become a kind of dark chant running through the subtext of our culture, from TV ads to popular songs to op-ed articles in newspapers and magazines. What is it about life in America today that drives us to push the ragged edge of danger in what were once our recreational pastime pursuits?

Whether or not you count yourself among these doldrum-defying daredevils, drag racing may not be your cup of tea. The criticisms to be laid at its gate are manifold, from pollution of the environment and depletion of nonrenewable resources to the exploitation of women and the encouragement, subliminal or otherwise, of drinking and driving way too fast. But the way I see it, the racing sports' shirtless, sunburned, beer-swilling, tobacco-spitting devotees are of the same stripe in their desire for intensity of experience as those who dress in phosphorescent spandex bodysuits and suckle Evian from plastic squeeze bottles while riding through suburbs on their fifteen-speed bicycles, not to mention those who wear lime-green pants and sun-yellow Izods and tipple Old Fashioneds between rounds of smacking tiny little balls at a very small hole a long ways off. There's just no accounting for taste.

Those who pride themselves on being open-minded in matters of race, sexual orientation, and politics while looking down their noses at the redneck faithful who follow racing as their thrill of choice may well suffer from self-deprivation, a malady I've heard described as "contempt prior to investigation." As the first step toward a remedy, I would make one observation and two suggestions: first, if you've never seen the flames, heard the roar, and felt the raw power of racing, you don't know what you're missing; second, do not despise what you cannot understand; and third, don't knock it 'til you've tried it—or at least heard the testimony of someone who has.

AT the awards ceremony held on the starting line after the final races on Sunday, Darrell Gwynn drove himself up onto the podium in a motorized wheelchair to be recognized for his continuing role in the sport of drag racing. Until a crushing accident during an exhibition run in England a couple of years before, Darrell was one of the fastest Top Fuel drivers of all. This day, however, he had only one arm and could not walk, yet still owned one of the most competitive racing teams in the country.

And there he was, sitting in the bright sunshine alongside the track chaplain, the race queen Miss Winston, and the top drivers in the sport, ten of the quickest men on the planet, smiling broadly, accepting no pity, encouraging others to take part in a sport to which he had given the better part of his life as well as a not-so-proverbial pound of flesh. While he waved to the rowdy crowd, I clapped for a moment along with everyone else, black, white, blue-collar, white-collar, and every redneck in between. Then I moved over closer to Frank so I could put one hand on little Jimi Dean's head and the other on James's rock-hard shoulder, and I held onto them just as tight as I could.

PAPA Hemingway said, "Mountain climbing, auto racing, and bullfighting are the only true sports . . . all others are games." Maybe you think he's mistaken on all three points, or you might just think he's wrong, period. But there's no denying the recent meteoric rise of auto racing as one of America's major entertainment industries. Gone are the days when ESPN's pretty boys announced the winner of each stock car race with a sneering wisecrack in an idiotic imitation of a Southern drawl. Nowadays the vast popular appeal of racing, and perhaps more to the point the sheer millions of dollars at stake every week on the racing circuit, have forced such media outlets as ESPN to give the sport its due, no matter how humble its beginnings or countrified its original fan base may have been. Even academic scholars and other cultural critics have begun to take a nuts-and-bolts look at the traveling circus that is American auto racing, peering beyond the beer-swilling, Confederate flag-waving, redneck stereotypes to investigate and chronicle the subculture of stock car competition.

There are those who study NASCAR, for instance, as a business generating millions of dollars in revenue, particularly if one includes the money that changes hands week by week through gambling, legal or otherwise. The race cars themselves are two-hundred-mile-per-hour billboards, splashed from bumper to bumper with a decal for each sponsor, the largest shelling out millions of dollars to field a race team for a single season. Add to all this seven-figure television and radio revenues, and what you have is a capitalist feeding frenzy growing so fast the sport itself cannot keep up. Older racetracks are adding thousands of seats to accommodate blue-collar fans in aluminum grandstands as well as luxury suites, even condominiums, for the well-to-do.

For the sake of such rapid growth, however, one must ask if NASCAR is selling its soul. A lower-class sport from its birth in the mountains of North Carolina and Virginia, where bootleggers souped up their jalopies to outrun the revenuers all week and each other on the weekends, stock car racing now finds its fan base shifting toward the upper middle class. Walk the Charlotte Motor Speedway parking lot on race day, and you'll find almost as many Beemers and Benzes as pickup trucks and hot rods. Unfortunately, with progress all too often comes inequity. Ticket prices are soaring, from $90 to $190 just to sit in the bleachers at Darlington, for instance.

The most shameful act on the part of NASCAR officials has been to shut down smaller, less profitable tracks in order to shift their race dates to huge new facilities in Las Vegas and Phoenix, with plans for even larger racing complexes in the near future. As I drove through North Wilkesboro, North Carolina, a few years back on my way to Merlefest, the annual bluegrass festival, it broke my heart to see the shutdown racetrack sitting empty as a crypt by the side of the road like a gigantic toy tossed aside by a spoiled child. Whenever the locals spoke of the speedway, there was a wistfulness in their eyes and an anger in their voices, not unlike so many axed employees who know they have been screwed, no matter if it's called downsizing. As far as hundreds of local vendors are concerned, the fat cats of NASCAR stole the high point of their financial year, all for the sake of larger profits, though to hear the racing elite tell it, it's all about the fans. Despite some doubters, there seems to be a disturbing unanimity at every level of racing, from drivers and mechanics to owners and fans, that growth is gospel. So they rush headlong—racing is, after all, a worship of speed—oblivious to the coming apocalypse when the racing industry, like Pan Am or IBM, eventually collapses of its own weight.

Other observers are taking a hard look at race relations in a traditionally Southern, almost exclusively white sport, and the news is not good. Nor will it be, despite NASCAR's recent efforts at diversity, until a minority driver—racing's Jackie Robinson, if you will—makes a breakthrough. Then there are the women, "racing widows" who live vicariously through husbands who build, drive, and repair extremely expensive toys, the young girls who hawk cigarettes and other wares in flimsy outfits, and the many thousands of females, around 40 percent of the fans, to whom racing seems to give satisfaction without representation. From time to time there are glimmers of hope, however, in terms of race, ethnicity, and gender, when minority drivers like Shauna Robinson or Bill Lester battle the odds and approach the threshold of full-time NASCAR racing.

But no fan is worthy of the name unless he or she is willing to venture out of the skyboxes and garages to rub elbows with the Great Unwashed. Anthropologists who in bygone days journeyed into the jungles of Africa and South America to spend time as participant/observers among the natives will find ample material for study should they dare drink cheap beer on Charlotte's Redneck Hill with the rowdy crowd of shirtless men and halter-topped women howling down the moon, or wander through the motor homes of nomadic fans who follow racing from track to track like Deadheads on their hippie *hijra*. The high and holy hour, after all is said and done, written and discussed, is still as ever the ritual of the race itself: the awesome speed, the bone-wracking noise, the fury of a pit stop. And then there are the accidents, as much a part of the spectacle of racing as the checkered flag, altogether a high-speed drama played out before a small city of shouting citizens.

There is a thin line, if any at all, between a fan and a fanatic. Witness all those decals you've seen but perhaps never thought about in the back windows of Chevy trucks, depicting an evil-eyed little boy urinating on the oval Ford symbol or, if it's in the window of a Ford pickup, spraying the Chevy bow tie. Racing's legacy can be read in its heroes, whose names true fans can recite like little Baptist children know the books of the Bible: Parsons, Petty, Earnhardt, and the more recent *wunderkind*, Jeff Gordon. Until his death, faithful Earnhardt fans pulled as hard against Gordon as they did for their own

man, and vice versa. These days Dale's son Junior has
taken up the cross to follow in his father's footsteps.

Other popular sports have for some time been given
close attention in intellectual circles. Such studies can
shed light on the deeper dimensions of racing not only
as a sport and a pastime but also as a telling phenomenon of human behavior. One observer, for instance,
teases out an intriguing comparison between racing and
baseball.[1] Both are as much fun to follow on the radio
as to watch on television, since the mind can visualize
the contest through the intensity of the commentators'
voices set against the noise of the spectators. Both can be
heard as a kind of background music with long stretches
of soothing monotony interrupted by sudden bursts of
excitement: "There's a long fly ball!" or "Trouble in Turn
Two!" Finally and most telling, it may well be that baseball, which is after all played in a grassy field, grew in
popularity out of a nostalgia for America's agrarian
roots at a time when our society was plunging headlong
into the urban, mechanical age. Now racing, obsessed as
it is with the internal combustion engine, evokes a similar nostalgia for the relative simplicity of machines even
as the digital age makes computer geeks of us all.

Frustrating though this may be, racing is like one of
those novels you love but know in your heart can never
be translated fully to film. Tom Wolfe's groundbreaking
if not prophetic essay "The Last American Hero" not-

---

[1] Scott Huler, *A Little Bit Sideways: One Week Inside a NASCAR
Winston Cup Race Team* (Osceola, WI: MBI, 1999).

withstanding, the definitive racing piece has yet to be written. So let me ask which you would rather do: read about baseball, or eat peanuts and Cracker Jacks while you sit with friends in the sun and watch the boys of summer play an honest-to-God game. As for racing, you can read books like the one you now hold in your hands either as an introduction to an eccentric subculture or to gain a deeper appreciation for a sport you already know and love, or you can sit yourself smack down in the middle of a NASCAR race. I see no reason why the best option couldn't be "All of the above."

CHAPTER FIVE

Gathering the Lost Sheep

I f you have ever witnessed a car wreck or arrived on the scene of an accident just after the collision occurred, the wheels of an overturned auto still spinning, smoke billowing from a busted motor, churned-up dust not yet settled, you might feel as if you can smell the chaos and carnage of unexpected impact. Such extreme situations divide us into distinct groups: some avert their eyes, cover their mouths, and cry, "Oh my God," while others simply stand and gawk, and then there are those who rush in to help. In the aftermath, whether among the witnesses, the victims, or perhaps even the helpers, someone will need a comforting hand and a reassuring voice to help them deal with what they have just been through. Likewise, in the dangerous world of stock car racing, where accidents are much more the norm than the exception, there are those who step forward in the face of tragedy to offer solace, to say, "I know you're shaken and afraid, but there is a bigger picture here. You may not feel it now, but everything is going to be all right."

Despite the Church's countless failings in the face of human suffering down through the centuries, an essen-

tial element of the high calling of Christianity is to offer
help to those in need. Although you might never know
it from the rantings of most television evangelists and
the shallowness of far too many Sunday sermons, the
teachings of Jesus deal much more with aiding widows
and orphans and those in distress than with condemning
sin or seeking the comforts of Heaven. Responding to
Jesus' counsel to spread this ministry of help and hope
to all in need, some Christians have taken the good news
all the way to the racetrack. Indeed, what better place to
find folks who are faced with the problem of evil, where
sidestepping danger is the only way to the winner's circle and every driver who finishes a race has won another
victory against the forces of death?

NASCAR's first chaplain was anything but official. A
converted hell-raiser by the name of Bill Frazier, affectionately called Brother Bill, was the first to catch a vision of the vast multitude of unsaved souls that has come
to be known as the NASCAR nation. Before his day, religious folk had at best ignored racers and their fans and
at worst condemned them for their sinful ways down at
the racetrack, drinking, cussing, betting—and all on the
Lord's day! "You might as well dance," says author Jerry
Bledsoe, his tongue firmly planted in his cheek. "It was
the devil's doings. That whole stock car racing crowd
was bound straight for hell."[1] Frazier, the prodigal son

---

[1] Jerry Bledsoe, *The World's Number One, Flat-Out, All-Time
Great, Stock Car Racing Book* (Garden City, NY: Doubleday, 1975),
216.

of a Baptist deacon, had wasted his youth barhopping and bed-hopping until one night in 1967 when he experienced what appears to have been a classic evangelical Christian conversion in which one is touched by God, as it were, and transformed in one's very being from wretchedness to righteousness. According to Frazier, "I'd tried everything else and failed, you know; I mean, I'd tried friendship, confided in people, tried sex, women, drinkin'. . . . When I really made up my mind, I asked God to help me. My life just changed. I got up the next day with a different outlook on life, started getting things back together."[2] What he got together was a gospel quartet and a pickup truck for a pulpit and showed up at the second race ever at what is now known as the Talladega Superspeedway in the spring of 1970. As fate would have it, however, Frazier's first attempt to convert the masses was rained out.

His second attempt, this time in the infield at Daytona on the Fourth of July, went off as planned, except for the fact that no one paid much attention to the pickup truck preacher. If you've ever seen street preachers barking at the passersby, I think you can understand why. But one thing about Brother Bill: he never gave up. Quite the contrary. The man went home, bought a flat-bed trailer, built a small wooden chapel on it, and hauled his creation to Talladega for the fall race that same year. His congregation that first day was not exactly a multitude; rather, only seven souls showed up, but for Brother

---

[2] Quoted in ibid., 218.

Bill it was a start. "Auspicious beginnings" might be more the term, because for everyone who attended the service, thousands more read about Brother Bill in newspapers carrying the latest racing news. According to Bledsoe, Brother Bill even showed up in *Sports Illustrated*, where he offered a quote that has turned out to be prophetic as to the relationship of current ministries with the corporation that is NASCAR, and more ominously the uncritical attitude of many American evangelicals toward right-wing conservative politics and a comfort level with getting and spending that seems anything but Christlike: "You see Goodyear, Prestone, Grey-Rock, and just about everything else you can think of at these races. I figured it was time the Lord got a little representation. I'm going to promote God just like the other guys promote STP."[3] In a sport where the racers' vehicles have been described as rolling billboards, God, it seems, is in danger of becoming one more product to be advertised.

And sure enough, some five years ago at a race in Darlington, driver Morgan Shepherd placed a Jesus decal on the hook of his car hauler, which NASCAR officials first had him remove due to complaints and then restore after countercomplaints from Christian fans. Shepherd's motivation for showing such stickers is not unlike that of other Christians who wear crosses or Jesus T-shirts: "When I display it on the hood of my car and these people see it, maybe somebody's life will be

---

[3] Ibid., 220.

changed."[4] The driver has taken his evangelical advertising scheme to a new level since 2001, when he formed his Victory in Jesus racing team. Perhaps the only surprise here, given stock car racing's Bible Belt birthplace and politically conservative climate, is that such an open expression of faith took so long to appear.

Meanwhile, back at the chapel, like the circuit-riding preachers of the nineteenth century, Brother Bill joined the caravan of pilgrims who to this day follow the racing circuit cross-country to join with local fans at each race. Some of the most fun I have ever had on the highway was the Saturday night I left Martinsville Speedway, ears still ringing from the roar of the race and throat sore from screaming, only to find myself caught up and carried along in a river of RVs, eighteen-wheelers, pickups, SUVs, restored roadsters, and motorcycles cascading down Route 220 toward the next race in Atlanta.

Replacing his rolling chapel with a tent—he was, after all, a revivalist—Brother Bill's nonjudgmental attitude eventually gained him the acceptance of the drivers and crews and, what's more, the racing powers that be. Eventually he was asked to pray at the close of one of the weekly prerace drivers' meetings. It was not long before his worship services spilled out of the tent and into the open air. Confirmation came that he was indeed what

---

[4] Dan Harris, ABC News Original Report, "NASCAR Takes Religion to the Raceway: Evangelical Faith Has Prominent Place in Nation's Fastest-Growing Spectator Sport," May 4, 2005, http://abcnews.go.com/WNT/story?id=727941&page=1 (accessed January 29, 2007).

many had begun to call him, the chaplain of stock car racing, when in the spring of 1972 the public address speakers at Talladega Superspeedway broadcast his sermon not only to the infield but also to the fans gathering in the grandstands. The rest, as they say, is history.[5]

Brother Bill Frazier was one of the first to build a bridge between the hell-raisers and the holy ones. Although criticized by church folk for fraternizing with unbelievers—one thinks of Jesus among the sinners and tax collectors—Frazier's ministry was an essential ingredient in washing away the stains of stock car racing's bad reputation. The financial advantages of this rebirth in respectability, and the broader public appeal that came with it, were not lost on Bill France or racing's other bigwigs.

OF all the many Christian ministries that have sprung up around the sport of racing since Brother Bill Frazier's time, Motor Racing Outreach is by far the most powerful, widespread, and influential. The organization boasts an annual operating budget of around $3 million, much of which is donated by drivers, car owners, sponsors, and churches to support MRO ministries among the NASCAR nation. In addition to NASCAR, MRO has grown to offer services to twenty other racing organizations, including International Race of Champions (IROC), Automobile Racing Club of America (ARCA), American

------

[5] I owe Jerry Bledsoe a debt of gratitude for this portrayal of Bill Frazier and his work.

Motorcycle Association, and American Power Boat Association, among others. "If it's got a motor on it and it races," says MRO chaplain Dale Beaver, "we try to have a chaplain there."[6] In the opening line of its slick brochures, MRO touts itself as "a multi-dimensional, non-profit 501(c)(3) organization" and goes on to claim that its role is "to undergird the racing family so that they may enjoy a more wholesome life together and, in turn, become positive role models for thousands of race fans at the track and around the world." As we shall see, the full extent of the relationship between MRO and racing organizations such as NASCAR may not be as simple as their publications might lead one to believe. Witness the highly prized monopoly over other ministries MRO's chaplains enjoy in terms of direct access to drivers, otherwise closely guarded and hard to come by. Nonetheless, this organization doubtlessly makes life at the track easier in many ways for the racers and fans who avail themselves of the ministry's offerings.

Think of NASCAR's Nextel Cup Series as a kind of traveling circus, a mobile village crisscrossing the continent from town to town and state to state for thirty-five of the fifty-two weekends in a year, and within this village live the same folks, car owners, drivers, pit crews, and support staff. Moreover, each racetrack is a buzzing

---

[6] Amy Sims, FoxNews.com, "Bowing Heads at the Ballpark," June 7, 2002, www.foxnews.com/printer_friendly_story/0,3566,54683,00.html (accessed January 29, 2007).

beehive of noise and motion all centered on an activity that is both intense and dangerous. In such a frantic atmosphere even the practiced Buddhist might find peace and quiet hard to come by. Add to this the fact that on most weekends the racing schedule climaxes on the Lord's day, and you can see why those racing pilgrims who are religious might come to miss the solitude of a silent sanctuary.

Into this void stepped Motor Racing Outreach. You might say MRO was born on a wish and a prayer. For some time during the 1980s, three now-retired drivers—Darrell Waltrip, Lake Speed, and Bobby Hillin—along with their wives, had been gathering together on a regular basis to provide one another support through the hectic racing season, all the while wishing for someone who could offer spiritual guidance not only to them but to others in the racing family as well. Lake Speed recalls, "We wanted our own church that went with us where we were going since we couldn't be in church on Sundays. We felt led that that's what God wanted as well, and we began praying as the three couples for months [that] God would help us get that established."[7] Their prayers for leadership were answered when in the spring of 1988 Waltrip and Speed met with a Tennessee-born, California-based race fan and Baptist preacher by the

---

[7] Steve Sharbutt, AgapePress, "Revin' Up for Revival: Motor Racing Outreach Provides Church away from Home," June 10, 2002, http://headlines.agapepress.org/archive/6/102002a.asp (accessed January 29, 2007).

name of Max Helton who himself had noticed the lack of adequate Christian ministry at the races he had attended.

Helton accepted the drivers' invitation to travel along the racing circuit and began hosting weekly Bible studies wherever he stayed. The turnout quickly outgrew his hotel rooms, and so in the summer of 1988 Helton led the first MRO worship service at Pocono International Raceway. These services grew to the point where Helton recently estimated that as many as 75 percent of the drivers attend, in addition to some owners and crew members. To this day MRO chaplains plan and oversee twenty- to thirty-minute worship services, typically evangelical affairs including the singing of traditional hymns or contemporary Christian songs and a short sermon sandwiched between opening and closing prayers. Attendance is usually limited to those who choose to linger after the drivers' meeting, a kind of pep rally and rulebook refresher course that takes place shortly before the race at each track. Allow me to share a brief account of one such service I attended a few years back.

It's getting on toward evening, and a full moon hangs over the darkened mountains huddled like huge sleeping beasts all around. I am one of a hundred or so souls who have gathered in this quiet place amid the bedlam of Bristol Motor Speedway. We are surrounded by 160,000 rowdy souls hooting and hollering as they wait for the green flag to drop and the mayhem to begin in the Sharpie 500. But for the next thirty minutes, the infield media center, a white cinder-block square set down in the center of the track like Islam's Kabah shrine in a Meccan courtyard, will serve as a solemn sanctuary where men and women bow their heads and quietly pray for courage and safety during the hectic hours to come. I can feel the tension in the room, like a fog of fear mingled with hope and dogged determination. The rows of metal folding chairs are full of racing's all-stars, yet no cameras are clicking, no recorders rolling. All eyes are on Dale Beaver, MRO chaplain, who stands before us speaking words of encouragement and caution like an officer addressing soldiers before battle. His confidence seems contagious, especially since he is saying out loud what everyone must be thinking but no one dares to believe, what each of us face every day of our lives and so few are willing to consider: there is danger here, and someone sitting in this room right now might be hurt; in fact, it could well be that not all of us will make it home tonight.

Beaver introduces Geoff Moore, a tall, stocky man with a soft voice and an acoustic guitar strung over one shoulder. Moore tells a sentimental story of lifting up his daughter, Anna, a Chinese toddler he and his wife adopted as an infant, and then realizing that in the same way he was cradling this child in his arms, keeping her safe from the troubles of a dangerous world, God was holding him. Perhaps tipping his hand toward a political stance on the issue of abortion, he ends the tale by saying, "God is in the adoption business."

Gently strumming his guitar, Moore dedicates a tune to the recently deceased Adam Petty with the words, "This song was a part of Adam's life." The music has the light air of pop, but the message is heavy and direct: when all is said and done, Jesus will be waiting on the other side. The word "death" is never spoken in the song or at any other time during the service, but there is no doubt what this gathering of souls is all about. When that inevitable moment comes and the Angel of Death calls their names, these folks want to be ready.

IN addition to serving as MRO's first chaplain, Max Helton, who has bowed his head in prayer with some of NASCAR's most famous drivers—Jeff Gordon, Kyle Petty, and Mark Martin, to name a few—is also the one most responsible for first taking MRO's brand of outreach to other forms of racing. Of all the MRO chaplains, however, Kentuckian Dale Beaver is the most widely known. He stood with Michael Waltrip in the 2001 Daytona 500 winner's circle when Beaver's wife shared the news that Earnhardt had wrecked and that it looked bad. He was also there in the hospital at the younger Earnhardt's side when Junior first learned of his father's death. And it was Beaver on whose shoulders fell the daunting task of giving the eulogy for Earnhardt during a televised memorial service in Charlotte, North Carolina's massive Calvary Church, which was attended by the Earnhardt family along with NASCAR's greater and lesser stars, and watched by millions more in homes, businesses, and bars. With calls from *People* magazine and *The Today Show* not long after the service, Beaver found himself caught up in the media frenzy following close on the heels of Earnhardt's death and broadening the NASCAR fan base, not to mention MRO's mission field, more than anyone in or out of racing could ever have dreamed.

Talk about a circuit-riding preacher: in a donated motor home Beaver and his wife and two sons join in the annual coast-to-coast NASCAR pilgrimage. Once he and his family arrive at a track, Beaver not only oversees the weekly prerace worship service but also engages in many of the same duties a less itinerant pastor would perform: premarital as well as other counseling, weddings, and funerals. Oftentimes when he is not away from his Charlotte home at a race, he pays weekday visits to the many race-team garages located in or near the Tarheel heart of racing country.

I have long argued in my classes that religions generally speaking and evangelical Christians in particular show much more concern for the well-being of our souls than they do for helping us live better lives in our bodies here and now. All too often, when evangelical groups offer food, clothing, and shelter to the poor and needy, it is as a lure to get these unfortunates to hear the gospel message of eternal life in the spirit, never mind what happens to the sinful, carnal body. There is no such thing as free alms, it seems. Once again, even a casual reading of the actual Gospels of the New Testament will show a Jesus much more concerned with providing practical help to his people on how to live in this world than with guaranteeing their souls go to Heaven at death and not Hell, as most evangelicals would have us believe.

Although MRO's ministries for the most part fit this unfortunate mold of placing more emphasis on the next life than on our present existence, one area where they offer comfort not only to souls but to bodies is through a mobile fitness and rehabilitation unit sponsored by Wake Forest University Baptist Medical Center. Here's the deal: the Medical Center provides operational funds in exchange for advertising exposure and public appearances by drivers for promotional purposes. Housed in a fifty-one-foot white trailer truck, the MRO Fitness Center and Rehab Unit is fully equipped with exercise bikes, weights, and massage benches. The professionally trained staff offers drivers and crew members a full program of rehabilitation services, everything from back and neck rubs to wrapping sore joints to more extensive physical therapy and fitness education.

The rehab unit was the brainchild of its current director, Bill Nelson, whose specialty is mechanical kinesiology or, to put it in plain English, the study of how the human skeleton and muscles work and how to maximize physical movement. Nelson had been studying the negative effects on drivers of both dehydration—think of driving in a cockpit at 150 degrees for four hours on a summer afternoon in Darlington—and the muscle fatigue that comes with wrestling a steering wheel, gear shift lever, and brake and clutch pedals at almost two hundred miles per hour. The powers that be at MRO took to his proposal of providing on-site therapy services and sent the rehab unit on its maiden voyage in 1999. Many's the grateful driver who can attest to just how good Bill Nelson's idea was.

An event known as the January Caution was begun in the mid-1990s by Jackie Pegram, co-coordinator of MRO's Women's and Children's Ministry. The "January" part is self-explanatory; the "Caution" signifies a break in the action, a time to slow down and catch a breath between racing seasons, which unlike most professional sports' schedules stretch from February into November. The annual event, attended by hundreds of the wives of racers and crew members, affords a chance for fellowship, an evangelical version of schmoozing, networking, and all-around enjoyment of one another's company. The gathering culminates with a catered dinner for which tickets have been sold, followed by the distribution of door prizes provided free of charge by local businesses. As Pegram put it, "We do a whole lot of laughing and a whole lot of praying, and we even sing."[8] She herself at times has spoken to the group, which usually gathers in one of Charlotte's fancier hotels, and took one opportunity to offer advice on how a "racing widow," literal or figurative, can hold on to her faith in the midst of the maelstrom that is a typical racing weekend.

However much the January Caution may help the women of NASCAR, the most important contribution Jackie Pegram makes to their quality of life is through ministering to their children. As far back as the 1980s Pegram couldn't help but notice the many drivers' and pit crews' youngsters playing in the track infields all those Sunday mornings before a race. Determined that these

---

[8] Liz Allison, NASCAR.com, "Caution Still Flying Along," January 16, 2002, www.nascar.com/2002/NEWS/01/16/allison _column/index.html (accessed January 29, 2007).

little ones should have the opportunity to learn the Bible's many stories even if no one could take them to a local church, in 1990 Pegram responded to Jesus' request as recorded in the Gospel of Mark, "Suffer the little children to come unto me," by sitting down with the sons and daughters of racing folks for a Bible study. Thus began what has come to be known as the Motor Racing Outreach Kids' Club. For lack of a better spot, that first gathering took place in the back of driver Phil Parson's car hauler, though nowadays the Kids' Club meets at almost every race in the MRO motor home, which doubles as a kind of community center.

The club, divided into two groups by age, usually includes anywhere from thirty to forty younger children and as many as twenty teens, who in addition to hearing Bible stories and life lessons also enjoy singing, playing games, and learning arts and crafts. The older group also takes part in activities away from the tracks from time to time, including summer camps, theme parks, rodeos, and the like. As weird as it must sometimes be to grow up as the child of a racing nomad, these youths seem happy to hang out with others from the same subculture.

What I find to be most fascinating about them is, generally speaking, an overall maturity, a sense of seriousness, compared with others their age. Finding oneself in a different town almost every weekend is bound to push a child to become more independent than others who live a more settled life, but I suspect their rapid development is due at least in part to growing up in an atmosphere of danger, playing hide-and-seek in the shadow of death, as it were. As Dale Beaver has said of racing's offspring, "They are very aware of the risks that are involved in the lives they live. They have a tremendous amount of faith because it's tested so much."[9]

Both inside the track and for miles around, a race sounds like one long lion's roar, as forty-odd V-8 engines rumble full throttle. Until the race is finished, any time that roar suddenly dies down, you know there's trouble somewhere on the track. It may be as minor as a piece of debris on the track or as serious as a twenty-car pileup. Whenever this relative silence shrouds the track, these children, like children everywhere, may not be able to see what is wrong or comprehend what it might mean, but they sense that all is not well and grow still and quiet. In such scary moments an adult will gather the children together and lead them in a word of prayer for the safety of all involved.

Not only does the Kids' Club offer these young pilgrims some consistency and a much-needed sense of normalcy, but also the ministry no doubt takes some of the pressure off mothers who would otherwise need to juggle making sure their children are out of trouble and entertained while at the same time trying to keep track of their husbands' safety throughout the race. And then of course these women might also enjoy having some time simply to be on their own.

---

[9] www.detnews.com/2001/motorsports/0108/17/h01-271717 .htm

I CAN still see his eyes, narrowed with suspicion, his lips a straight line, a locked barrier of fear and mistrust, and all because I had said the wrong words. I cannot tell you his name, because he told me I couldn't, but I will tell you that at the time we spoke, he was the director of Operations who supervised the chaplains for Motor Racing Outreach, the nation's largest Christian ministry aimed specifically at the sport of racing. He and I met in the MRO suite nestled in that great glass-and-shining-steel cathedral of stock car racing, the massive control center of the Charlotte Motor Speedway in Concord, North Carolina. He sat bolt upright on the far side of his desk in a cushy corner office, the bright blue spring sky beaming through the wall of windows to his back.

I had introduced myself and told him I was writing a book about God and NASCAR, seeking to explore the connections between religion and racing. It was when I used the term "religion" that a change came over him. He fixed me with a steely gaze, his voice flat but for a hint of compassion or pity, as he asked, "So what is your own personal relationship with the Lord?"

I should have seen it coming. I've spent years among the Baptists and in the days of my fundamentalist youth even put forth the same question to unsuspecting ears. It wasn't what he said but how he said it that caught me off guard and left me speechless a little too long for his liking. Kicking myself inwardly for being so ill-prepared, I fumbled and failed to find the right words to tell this stranger, who had confronted me with about as personal a question as one could ever ask, how I had become a Christian at the age of sixteen. Not long after, I came to see Jesus Christ as the one and only way to God. Yet through all these many years of studying the scriptures, history, and myths of the great religions, punctuated by an intense and agonizing struggle with the problem of evil, I had slowly grown into the realization that Christianity may well not be the only path to the divine, and what's more, that it might not even be the most interesting route.

So the interview was pretty much over before it had begun. He all but refused to answer my questions, insisted that I not use his name in my book, and asked whether or not my project was licensed by NASCAR. Years earlier, I might have stood to go, offered to shake his hand, and left. But it helped that I am familiar with his tactic of throwing someone else off guard by cutting to the evangelical chase. In his eyes, apparently, nothing was more important at that moment than the eternal well-being of my soul, and this belief justified sidestepping every rule of social politeness and even what some might call Christian cooperation to help another who has asked for what was his to give: at the very least, information, and above and beyond the call of duty, encouragement.

One of my most shameful moments as an evangelical Christian was participating in a Campus Crusade for Christ survey during my college years. Dozens of us were sent in pairs into the Furman University dorms to knock on doors and ask our fellow students to answer a few seemingly innocent questions. The unstated purpose of this survey, however, was to move from the most general queries about the participant's hometown and interests into probing intimate details on their personal relationship with God. If all went according to plan, the survey culminated in leading the participant to recite the simplistic recipe to which Campus Crusade has reduced the incredibly complex human experience of the Almighty, what founder Bill Bright has called the Four Spiritual Laws:

1. God loves you, and offers a wonderful plan for your life.
2. Man is sinful and separated from God. Therefore, he cannot know and experience God's love and plan for his life.
3. Jesus Christ is God's only provision for Man's sin. Through Him you can know and experience God's love and plan for your life.
4. We must individually receive Jesus Christ as Savior and Lord; then we can know and experience God's love and plan for our lives.[10]

The problem was that, although some students would follow our lead and walk through the survey, whether due to curiosity, personal need, or fear of not being polite, others sensed that we were not being straight up with them, and a few expressed their discomfort or disgust in no uncertain terms. Eventually I shied away from taking part in this deceitful practice, however well-

---

[10] Global Media Outreach, "The Four Spiritual Laws," http://www.greatcom.org/laws/ (accessed January 29, 2007).

intentioned it may have been, and stopped going to Campus Crusade meetings altogether.

So there I was decades later, in a fancy office in a state-of-the-art edifice, confronted by a similar form of well-intentioned, wrongheaded concern for my soul that would not hesitate to compromise my humanity for the sake of leading me into the Kingdom. But belligerence is not my style, and so you might say I killed him with kindness. The old Baptist preacher who still resides deep down inside me rose up; my voice took on that plaintive, sermonic cadence as familiar as an old hymn, and I assured this man in no uncertain terms that, though he and I might not see eye to eye on the details, my heart is right with God. By the end of the hour he had relaxed somewhat and even offered to share a little of the history of Motor Racing Outreach.

I wanted to ask the director to tell me his favorite racing tales, because I believe it is in people's stories where the most genuine truth lies, rather than in some supposedly objective perspective gained through observation and secondhand information. But all that went by the board when he sidetracked us for what he no doubt considered more important things. He did tell me that the role of racing chaplains is to give "care in times of stress," but I never got the chance to ask him if a particular race or specific wreck stood out in his mind.

Another question that unfortunately went unasked was whether there are chaplains for racers and their families and crews who might belong to religions other than Christianity, say, Jews or Muslims or even Catholics (considered by most evangelicals to be among the lost and therefore in need of salvation). If there are chaplains prepared to minister to folks of other faiths, they are certainly not on the MRO payroll. MRO might be multidenominational, but it is by no means interfaith. The organization's stated purpose is "to lead the racing community to personal faith in Christ, to growth in Christlikeness and to active involvement in a local church" (Motor Racing Outreach brochure).

MRO is to be commended for seeking not just to save souls but also to foster a relationship between believers and a local church where they can find fellowship and grow in their faith. Nevertheless, the MRO mission comes off as shortsighted if not downright ethnocentric, assuming as it does that Christianity, or rather a specific version thereof, is the supreme vision of divinity and one that cancels out all others. Admittedly, given the sport's Southern roots, it is not surprising that the vast majority of NASCAR folks, if they claim any religion at all, would be Christian and more specifically Baptist. Yet as the sport grows and its demographic broadens into the wider populace, there is no doubt an increasing need for more pluralistic, interfaith ministries.

AFTER I left the MRO offices and that near train wreck of an interview, I could not shake the sense of unease I had felt ever since the director of operations had buttonholed me with his impertinent question, as if a stranger had slipped his hand in my pocket, even if it was to make sure I had not locked the keys in my truck. Yet the feeling went deeper than that. In fact, I finally figured out that what had put me off about my time with this man was more than what he asked so bluntly. It was what he refused to say outright.

The longer we talked, the clearer it became that his number one concern was not that my soul was saved, nor even that my book or the chapter on Motor Racing Outreach be written from a Christian perspective, whatever that may mean and however he might define it. Rather he seemed bent on seeing to it that I not say anything to jeopardize the financially sweet relationship he and his organization have fashioned with the cash cow that NASCAR has now become. That all too cozy friendship between the Church and the marketplace, which flies in the face of Jesus' insistence that we cannot serve both God and money, cuts to the very root of the hypocrisy that drove me from the ranks of the Church all those many years ago.

The covenant between MRO and NASCAR is a multilayered one, and at the deeper levels one finds an ugly example of what has been called the dark side of religion, an adulterous affair between the bride of Christ and the whore of Babylon, a betrayal of the Everlasting One for the sinful succor of the Almighty Dollar. On the surface MRO lends an air of unquestionable integrity to NASCAR, and NASCAR gives MRO a sense of prestige. Underneath, however, MRO follows the NASCAR juggernaut like a feeder fish hovering oh so delicately underneath a shark, gaining access to millions of unchurched souls and untold amounts of tax-free monies.

At the same time, NASCAR can conceal its sins as a reckless sport (no pun intended) selling its soul to the highest bidder behind the Christian banner of MRO, as if to say, "See, we support family values, and we have the blessing of God."

On the air-conditioned elevator ride back down to ground level, I recalled with a sour lump in my throat the day my home church decided to spend a small fortune to build a recreation center with a full gymnasium for the church's youth while within a stone's throw from the future groundbreaking ceremony children went to bed hungry every night. And then there was the last church where I served as assistant pastor, shepherded—I kid you not—by the Reverend Good, where I labored to bring into the fold a dozen or so troubled but promising young men and received pats on the back from our relatively well-to-do deacons, that is, until those same "delinquents" started sitting with the deacons' daughters during the Sunday service. Shortly thereafter I narrowly lost in a vote of no confidence from the congregation, left that church as well as the Church more broadly understood, and never looked back. Stepping off the elevator, the bright Charlotte sun brought me abruptly back to the present moment, and before I climbed into my truck for the ride home, though the speedway parking lot was coated with asphalt as black as night, I still felt the need to kick the dust off my boots.

CHAPTER SIX

Pilgrimage to Memphis

One night while writing this chapter, I dreamed I walked onto the quaint little campus of Southeastern Baptist Theological Seminary in Wake Forest, North Carolina, where I graduated in 1981 with a Master of Divinity degree, and started calling down fire and brimstone. Not in the chapel, not in a classroom, but on the quad between the administration building and the library, right out in front of God and everybody. "Woe to you, Pharisees, hypocrites!" I cried. "You shut up the kingdom of heaven against your fellow humans, you devour widows' houses and for a pretense make long prayers; it is you who will receive the greater damnation." I was just getting warmed up.

A small crowd gathered at a respectful distance. Paige Patterson was there. In my waking moments I know that he is the former president of Southeastern Seminary and a spiritual disciple of W. A. Criswell, who served for fifty years as pastor of the First Baptist Church of Dallas, Texas, at one time under his leadership the largest church in the Southern Baptist Convention. Criswell was the spiritual father of the fundamentalist takeover of the Southern Baptist Convention during the time

I happened to be at Southeastern. Perhaps his most famous contribution to the fundamentalist cause is a book
whose influence on evangelicals, particularly those of
the Baptist stripe, can hardly be underestimated: *Why I
Preach That the Bible Is Literally True.* The title pretty much
says it all.

"Woe to you," I shouted. "Pharisees, hypocrites! You
cross sea and land to make one convert, and when he is
converted, you make him twofold the child of Hell that
you yourselves are. Woe to you, hypocrites, who pay
your tithes but omit the weightier matters of the law:
judgment, mercy, and faith. You blind guides, who
choke on a gnat but swallow a camel." By then it must
have been obvious to all gathered that I was not joking,
because the expressions on their faces were changing
from mild amusement to something darker, more sinis-
ter. I did not let up. "Woe to you, hypocrites! You white-
washed sepulchers, beautiful on the outside but inside
full of filthy dead men's bones. You may appear righteous, but within you are full of hypocrisy and iniquity."

Off to my right I saw, standing on the far side of the
low stone wall that separates the school campus from the
town of Wake Forest and the rest of the world, several
of the professors who had opened my mind to things
undreamt of while I was a student there. There was
B. Elmo Scoggin, the wiry old Hebrew teacher with the
patriarchal white beard and a crooked forefinger that
waved through the air like the curves of the Hebrew al-
phabet, the *alephs* and *beths* and *gimels* and *daleds* that he

drove us day after day to memorize. Dr. Scoggin stood shoulder to shoulder with the handsome young theologian Claude Stewart, who first blessed me with the idea that God might actually take an active part in the process of creation, changing and suffering and growing with the cosmos rather than standing in cold perfection over and above it like some alien Original Being. This realization was one of the turning points in my pilgrimage from a close-minded fundamentalist upbringing toward a more open, humane worldview. Having seen the writing on the wall soon after the fundamentalists took over the Convention and began purging from their ranks anyone who dared suggest that questioning long-held truths might actually be a more noble act of faith than acknowledging authority, Stewart like so many others left Southeastern Seminary to teach in less hostile environs. As stubborn as Moses to the bitter end, Scoggin toughed it out for a few years before retiring.

Like a somber Greek chorus, these two men stood there beyond the wall alongside the other professors who were scorned as liberals if not heretics. As far as I know, no one was fired exactly; the powers that came to be did it the old-fashioned way, by creating an environment of hostility and intimidation that eventually accomplished the goal of eradicating all but the most conservative faculty and staff. Their appointed replacements have been bright enough for the most part, but their scholarship seldom if ever fails to toe the party line of literally true scriptures and male domination in both

theology (God is definitely "our Father") and practice
(no female preachers). It was as if the Baptists adminis-
tered themselves a frontal lobotomy.

Glancing back into the crowd around me, I noticed
with that sense of weirdness so common in dreams the
portly jowls and beady eyes of Rush Limbaugh staring
out at me from the midst of the crowd. "How hard it
is for a rich man to enter into the kingdom of heaven!"
I shouted. "It is easier for a camel to go through the
eye of a needle than for the rich to enter into the kingdom of God. Blessed are the poor, for theirs is the kingdom of Heaven." Next to Rush glowed the cherubic face
of Ralph Reed, the glib poster boy of the Christian Coali-
tion. "Woe to you, hypocrites," I cried again. "You say
much, and do nothing. You lay unbearable burdens on
people's shoulders, but you yourself will not lift a finger
to help." Beside Reed the round mug of Pat Buchanan
laughed with eyes squeezed shut and mouth wide open.
"Love your enemies," I said. "Bless those who curse you,
do good to those who hate you, and pray for those who
despitefully use you, so that you may be children of God,
who makes the sun rise on the evil and on the good and
sends rain on the just and on the unjust. For if you love
only those who love you, what reward do you have?
Don't even lawyers do the same? And if you salute your
brothers only, don't even tax collectors do as much?" Buchanan's hysterical laughter spread like wildfire through
the crowd, all the while growing louder and louder until
it drowned out everything I tried to say. The more I

shouted, the louder they howled. The next thing I knew, I was sitting up in bed, sucking air, baptized in sweat.

To this day, I cannot get those faces out of my mind, and despite the public humiliation of almost every major player, I keep wondering what my dream might mean. I know that in ancient times, certain dreams were considered to be visions, prophecies not so much of the end of time in the far distant future as of impending events in days shortly to come. The Hebrew prophets, after whom Jesus patterned himself and of whom he was surely one, looked into such dreams and saw promises of hope as well as dire warnings. I sense very little hopefulness in my dream—or nightmare, as the case may be—but a definite warning. Caught off our guard in the late 1970s and early 1980s, the more moderate Baptist faculty, staff, and students stood by and watched as the religious right wing took control of the Seminary and turned it from a place of debate into a hall of indoctrination. All the while we were saying, "This cannot be happening here." By the time we had come to our senses and rallied to do something to stop the takeover, it was too late. The fundamentalists marshaled the numbers, giving them the power to do as they pleased. The rest, as they say, is hysterical.

Still shaken by the reality of my dream or vision or whatever it was, I cannot say much about the end of time, but I do have something to say about impending events in days shortly to come. Over the past twenty-five years, I have watched with both chagrin and a fair measure of disbelief as political fundamentalists rally the Christian soldiers before every election day. What began as a dogfight of biblical proportions—as Buchanan was so fond of saying, "for the heart and soul of the Republican Party"—now the compromises first made by the conservative elite to keep the so-called Christian right within the fold have led to an evangelical takeover of the nation's very government. Yet still I pray the vast majority of the American people, if they have not already done so, will realize before it is too late the inherent dangers of theocracy, the rule of God in human affairs, which is actually a domination by those confused and ruthless enough to claim that their limited view might actually be the will of an almighty creator of universes known and as yet unknown. The political and spiritual heirs of the Limbaughs and Reeds and Buchanans threaten to do to the American Republic what Criswell and Patterson and their pawns have done to Southeastern Seminary. If given their will, however much they might claim it to be the will of God, our nation will come under the rule of religious laws even more ancient and almost as strict as any version of Muslim sharia. Whatever you may think of their religion or their politics, it is plain to see these evangelicals mean business, and they are not going away.

Eternal vigilance is the price of liberty.

Lest some of my more religious readers think I am condemning Christianity as a whole or one sect in particular, follow me, if you will, on a recent pilgrimage into an adjoining area of this garden Flannery O'Connor called "the Christ-haunted South," to a tree with roots in the Southern past as deep and strong as any that nourish stock car racing. For it was on this journey that I came to see as never before the proven potential of evangelical Christians to do good in this world. I went on an expedition in search of the roots of American music, the blues, country and western, and gospel, but what I brought home was a mandate. The surprising message I heard loud and clear was this: when those who would follow in Jesus' footsteps apply courageously, even to the point of self-sacrifice, his message and example of challenging power, both political and religious, in order to help the poor and downtrodden, lives can be redeemed, societies revolutionized. As we shall see, though it may sound corny to say in this cynical age, sometimes a dream does come true.

On a cloudy August Sunday I told friends and loved ones good-bye, hoping it would not be for the last time, climbed on my Honda Shadow, pointed my handlebars west, and began the long haul from the eastern piedmont of North Carolina all the way to the Mississippi River. I was headed for Memphis, via Asheville and Nashville, in search of the headwaters of that blessed American blending of white and black, rural and urban, country and western, and rhythm and blues that has become the mighty river of rock 'n' roll. To paraphrase one of Elvis's most famous admirers, I had reason to believe we all will be received: I was going to Graceland.

Before I was old enough to know what music was, Mom and Dad were listening to Elvis Presley, born the year between their own births, sing "Mystery Train" and "Heartbreak Hotel" on the radio. In the early 1960s, after Dad had left for the second shift down at the mill, Mom would put on her scratchy old 45-rpm records and take turns dancing with my brothers and me across the living room rug. After Elvis's escape from Hollywood and all those cheesy movies, we sat on the couch together to watch his 1969 comeback special. Mom's sad eyes glowed like the faces of the beautiful groupies lounging around the stage where a tanned and trim Elvis strutted and sweated, his black leather suit as shiny as the velvet robes of Krishna.

Yet by 1977, when my housemate walked in one day and said, "The King is dead," I'd almost forgotten about Elvis, who had become for me a kind of Las Vegas circus clown. Since that time, however, Elvis has made yet another comeback. You've heard about, and perhaps experienced for yourself, the occasional sightings: he's down at the Waffle House ordering a grilled peanut butter and banana sandwich, or he's paying some poor woman's electric bill. There are Elvis impersonators of all ages and stripes, even El Vez, the Mexican Elvis, and Elvis Herselvis, a cross-dressing King/Queen of Rock 'n' Roll. The University of Mississippi has hosted an annual conference where postmodernist scholars of pop culture struggle to re-vision Elvis's sad, drugged-out demise in light of his earlier life, from the poverty of Tupelo to the magnificence of Memphis.

Now entering my own middle years and wondering how the hell I've become the person I am today, sifting through childhood memories in the writing of a novel and the intensive interchange of therapy, I've felt a growing need to know the man behind the icon, where Elvis came from, and why he streaked across the American sky like some mysterious comet. And so I traveled, like so many others, to visit his home. Little did I know I would find a land of grace, not at Elvis's sepulchral mansion, but a couple of miles and a thousand cultural lightyears away.

I ran into rain before I reached the county line and stopped alongside Interstate 85 long enough to throw on my rain suit. At the next exit I parked under the awning of a closed service station. I had no idea this brief stop to stay dry was a harbinger of things to come. By the time I finished my cigarette, the thundercloud had passed over, so I continued my climb up from the Appalachian foothills to Asheville, Land of the Sky.

My friends Junior James and Nancy were waiting for me there. We sat on their darkening porch with a bottle of Jose Cuervo and mourned the idiotic arsonist's torching of the Old Kentucky Home, the downtown boardinghouse run by Thomas Wolfe's mother and setting for much of *Look Homeward, Angel*. I asked, "What kind of defective mental machinery does it take to produce the thought, 'Hey, I think I'll go out tonight and burn down the Wolfe Memorial'?" Dear old Thomas was the first of many heroes dead far too young whom I would honor on my trek.

As night fell, we spoke of Nashville and Memphis and the religion of rock 'n' roll. Some time during the evening, my friends talked themselves into accompanying me by car as far as Nashville. Next morning, cups of caffeine washing away tequila cobwebs, they cranked up the car and we headed out for what with a ruler and a map I had surmised would be a five-hour ride. Little did I know how curvy the interstate highway is between Asheville and Knoxville, which is only about halfway to Nashville, so that five hours became six, seven, eight, the last two of which were excruciating, and there was nothing to do but endure.

The first hour of riding was a delight. There was no stereo or cell phone to distract me, so once I had worried about everything I could think of and sung every song I knew, my mind eventually emptied itself and became still. I entered a zone of astonishing quiet, not preoccupation or absentmindedness, but *presentmindedness*, a state of stark awareness of and openness to the world through which I was rapidly rolling. The grass and trees became somehow greener, the sky bluer, the air fresher and more invigorating, as though I had slipped into a shimmering Van Gogh landscape. Crossing over the French Broad River, that great mythic water of my youth, nature's beauty opened out into the sublime, tears welled up and were pushed back into my hair by the wind, and thick chunks of emotion heaved up in my throat. That moment was as near an experience of the divine presence, right down to my very bones, as I have ever come.

As the miles rolled on and the rapture wore off, the bike's constant vibration set up a soreness in my bones and sinews, so that every joint ached and the tendons began to burn like flames of fire. During the next hour, however, a soothing numbness set in, my mind hummed like a well-oiled engine, and my body somehow melded with the iron bones and rubber muscles of the bike. This peaceful state lasted for about two hours, and that's where the trouble began. Once the numbness wore off, demons of pain gnawed my flesh, and I was forced to take several rest stops to ensure sanity and safety.

Nevertheless the ride to Knoxville was the most exhilarating of the entire trip. I had never biked in the mountains before, and the slow ascent to Asheville had not prepared me for the twenty-mile-long roller-coaster ride down the far side of the eastern spine of our dromedary continent. I leaned into the curves bending on and on as if without end and ducked into tunnels blasted right through the gut of the oldest mountains on Earth.

Because the roadway was so unpredictable, concentration was never more important but difficult at best. For much of the downhill slalom, I could have reached out to the left and scraped my gloved fingertips on a solid cement dividing wall, while to my right twenty tons of roaring steel barreled by. The truck drivers almost always took note of this free bird winging along beside, much the way I do when, trapped in a rolling iron cage, I spy a fortunate soul soaring on two wheels with the wind in his or her face. A hand-painted sign stuck against the mountainside warned: REPENT—

LAST CALL, and I thought, *Wasn't that the last thing Frankie the barkeep told me before I left town?*

I shut my mouth tight to keep from swallowing sand and grit as I passed by the recently cleared spot where most of a mountainside had swept across the roadway, blocking traffic for weeks. Highway crews had strung great strands of hurricane fencing like bridal lace across the pocked face of the mountain to prevent further catastrophes. Oh, the folly of humanity, to think we could stop these ancient hills from crumbling back into the ocean where they arose all those eons ago, as if we are not speeding this inevitable process with our latest innovation: acid rain.

On I rode through the manic rush hour of Knoxville and down the leveling slope into the foothills tracing wrinkles in the tender old face of Mother Earth. Near the exit for Bucksnort, Tennessee, above me soared the largest hawk I have ever seen, with a wingspan as wide as my motorcycle is long. The sun leaned westward, bright star guiding my way, while muscular storm clouds moved like white-haired gods along the horizon. By the time I finally reached the outskirts of Nashville, that famous skyline shimmering like a dream in the distance, my fingers were all but frozen by fatigue, curved like claws from clutching the handlebar grips.

Music City was a hoot. I hooked up with my friends for a Mexican dinner, and we strolled down Broadway as dark settled in. Two pompadoured bohunks sat on the darkening corner by Ernest Tubb's Record Store strumming guitars and singing Merle Haggard for tips. Although it was Monday, all the bars were open, and a cacophony of country music accosted us. We stumbled into Celebrity's Corner, a shotgun shack of a bar, every wall plastered with album covers, country, rock, even disco. A five-piece band called F-Troop served up tasty cover tunes spiced with hot guitar licks. A gaggle of French teens requested "Whole Lotta Shakin' Goin' On," and they all danced like the Peanuts gang in loose-limbed abandon. When an older British gentleman stood and sang the late Conway Twitty's heartbreaker "It's Only Make Believe," the hyperactive hot dog lady who was working her food stand on the street stepped inside to pay quiet homage.

We lucked out, because Tuesday evening was bluegrass night at the Ryman Theater, former home of the Grand Ole Opry whose center stage holds a circle of wood cut from the stage of the Ryman and moved like a religious relic, a piece of the True Cross, to lend a brand of apostolic authenticity. In the lobby we paused for a moment before the bronze statue of Roy Acuff sitting with Minnie Pearl, then climbed to the balcony of that hallowed hall like bashful backseat Baptists. Along with a four-piece band in identical navy blue suits, longtime bluegrass stalwarts Jim and Jesse took the stage, their preternaturally dark hair coiffed to resemble soft black helmets—and rightfully so, since they butted heads throughout their set, bantering back and forth between "my big brother Jim" and "my little brother Jesse."

Much of it was good-natured horseplay, but enough sparks flew to prove that such sibling rivalries never really end.

Jim kept the rhythm on guitar while Jesse's virtuosic mastery of the mandolin showed the cold fingers of old age have yet to get a grip on him. It was heartening to see that Jesse's grandson has taken up the fiddle and joined the band. The old-time music, it seems, has a bright future after all. When they played John Prine's "Paradise," something of the sense of safety I felt as a child sitting in church, what the Baptists call "blessed assurance," came over me. I turned to my buddies and stage-whispered, "I've gone to Heaven without having to die."

The evening hit full swing with the Osbourne Brothers, both dressed to the nines. Sonny, the spitting image of Charlie Daniels from his ten-gallon hat to his tooled leather boots, emceed their set and frailed a mean banjo, while Bobby, a dead ringer for Truman Capote, sporting a crisp white suit and Panama hat, strummed his mandolin and fended off his brother's wisecracks. They opened with "Great Speckled Bird" and tore it up on the nostalgic "Georgia Mules and Country Boys":

> I'm not knockin' progress
> but it hurts me some to say
> Georgia mules and country boys
> are fadin' fast away

The fiddle interlude midway through "Farther Along" took my breath, but the spiritual high point of the evening was the brothers' soul-stirring harmonies on "Beneath Still Waters." In that silent moment after the song ended and before the clapping began, a chill ran right up my spine. Junior James leaned over and elbowed me. "If church was this good, I'd still be going!"

The next day we visited the Country Music Hall of Fame, somber monument to days and lives gone by. There was the letter written from jail by Lefty Frizzell to his sweetheart, with the original lyrics to "I Love You a Thousand Ways": "I love you, I'll prove it in days to come." All around were guitars and sequined suits like nothing I'd ever seen, all glitter and flash. And Lord have mercy, the cars: Webb Pierce's Lincoln limo customized with a horse saddle, Elvis's Cadillac with a wet bar and gold-plated record player in the backseat. It was saddening to see how few sat in the little theater for a touching documentary about the all too brief life and career of the Father of Country Music, Jimmie Rodgers.

For me the sacred center of the museum was the cavernous room dedicated to Hank Williams, the very first member of the Hall of Fame, with framed manuscripts of his original lyrics, like "I Saw the Lite," penned in the days before spell check. My eyes teared up as I read the telegram, a brief and devastating poem, from Hank's mother to his sister, "Come home. Stop. Hank is dead. Stop. Mama. Stop." Stepping back out into the sunlight, I felt less like a tourist than a pilgrim who had finally made it to Mecca. Something deep inside, a sacred seed planted in me as a little boy by my own mama's daddy, who listened to George Jones and Tammy Wynette, Porter Wagoner and Dolly Parton on the dashboard radio in his '63 Chevy, had come to fruition, and in my soul I felt truly blessed.

We did the bar crawl again that night down on Broadway, and the next day we packed up to go. My friends headed back toward Asheville, and once again I went west toward what I thought was the ultimate goal of my journey, Graceland. Once I hit the open country-side, I stopped for gas at one of the thousands of little convenience stores stuck smack in the middle of every American nowhere. There was a beefy guy in a skullcap helmet straddling a Harley at the other pump, and when I threw my leg over the tank to stand, he pulled up beside me and gunned his engine. "Now why would you buy one of *them* when you could have one of *these*?"

I rolled my eyes behind opaque shades. *Oh, brother,* I thought, *not again.* "So what're you riding?" I asked him, trying and failing to keep the edge out of my voice.

"Sportster. Probably cost less than that thing."

No, and this thing doesn't leak oil. "Nice bike," I offered. "My brother rode a Sportster back in the day."

He snorted. "At least one of you's got good sense."

I'd punch you right square in the nose, pal, but I'm headed for an audience with the King. "Well, I've been riding straight through for three days, and she hasn't missed a lick."

"Is that the 1100?"

Does it really make your bike more enjoyable if you throw off on somebody else's? My voice came out pinched like water spewing through a leak. "No, it's a 600, and it fits me like a glove." I glanced up at the store window to see if there were any witnesses, in case he couldn't find it in himself to let it go. "I'm shooting for Memphis, going to Graceland. How about you?"

"Oh, I'm headed right down the road here. The old lady's waiting."

"Nice talking to you. Keep it between the ditches."

He finally smiled. "Rubber side down, dude." He gunned the motor again and kicked up gravel on his way out of the parking lot. *Lord, have mercy,* I thought as I watched him go, *what's it like to be you?* I went in and bought a Gatorade, sat down on the curb, and smoked a cigarette until my nerves quit jangling.

Once I settled back into the ride, something in my body, a tightness in the muscles across my forehead and down either side of my spine, told me I was heading into uncharted territory. That's when a mantra from my childhood, a plaintive hymn Dad's mom Mamaw Russell always hummed, started up in my head: "Lord, I'm one, Lord, I'm two, Lord, I'm three, Lord, I'm four, Lord, I'm five hundred miles away from home." Somewhere in that lonely stretch of asphalt, trees, and overpasses be-tween Nashville and Memphis, the country music capital and the city of the blues, I realized that somehow I've managed to outlive Elvis, not to mention dear ol' Hank, Jimmie Rodgers, and countless other pioneers, black and white, who spent their short lives creating this musical phenomenon we take so much for granted. I knew full well that one wrong move by another driver could bring my own life to an abrupt end, but I pressed on, drawn as if by instinct to the darker heart of American music.

It was only when I was tooling past Jackson, Tennessee, that I learned from a historical marker that here was the hometown of recently deceased Carl Perkins. It pained me to pass up the opportunity to pay him homage, but I was already behind schedule, noisy storm clouds were threatening rain any moment, and stopping was out of the question. So I blew the old rocker a kiss and promised I'd think of him whenever I wore my blue suede Hush Puppies. Somehow I had the feeling the untiring rock 'n' roll trooper would understand if I kept right on rolling.

In Memphis, I checked into a motel right down by the Big Muddy, and as soon as I stowed the bike under the portico and tossed my bags on the bed, I walked out to the riverside, hunkered down by a weeping willow, and watched the water rushing by until hypnotized by the vast sight and sound of it. No wonder the beautiful, breathing Mississippi holds a mythical stature like no other natural phenomenon in American culture: it's a river so wide even George Washington couldn't toss a silver dollar across it.

Satisfied that I had reached the westernmost point of the pilgrimage, my own personal Mecca, I showered off the road dust and headed down to party central, Beale Street. The first thing I saw was a sign pointing the way to the Civil Rights Museum. *Note to self*, I thought. *Be sure you check that out before you go.* I parked just off Beale, and before I could even get my gloves off, I was accosted by a scruffy young black man offering an armful of flowers. Caught by surprise and still shell-shocked from the day's ride, I jerked off my helmet and barked a guilty, "No!" The man looked at me like I had called him a dirty name before storming off down the street toward a cluster of giggling yuppies. In my head I heard Jack Nicholson say, "Auspicious beginnings."

Yet as I walked the length of this legendary street, a classic American avenue Edward Hopper might have painted, past souvenir shops and bars already blaring the blues at two in the afternoon, I wasn't sure who were more troublesome, the most aggressive panhandlers I've ever encountered, perched on park benches like vultures waiting for a struggling beast to die, or the thick clots of "tourons" refusing to offer them a trickle-down dime for the service they provide: helping the Other Half feel smug and superior, if not safe, in their police-patrolled and gated suburban communities.

I stepped into a rib joint on the corner and found myself unable to hear a word the waitress was saying as she tried to take my order. My ears were ringing like a four-alarm fire and I was all but deaf from 750 miles worth of wind whipping through my head. Fortunately, being hard of hearing was no problem, since the blues were blasting wherever I went, and everybody yelled to be heard. Soon enough, the waitress brought me a steaming plateful of baby back ribs, crisp along the edges and juicy up next to the bone. As my dad would say, these ribs were so good they'd make your tongue slap your brains out.

For two nights I stumbled from one bar to another, soaking up all the blues I could find, most of which was played, in this town like any other in America, by white guys faking it. Even Jim Beam couldn't convince me otherwise. You know you're in a bad way when it's the absence of the blues and not the blues themselves that depresses you. Nevertheless, there was one incandescent moment, a musical epiphany I cannot forget: in a smoky bar called the Black Diamond, a chubby old blues master by the name of Blind Mississippi Willie Morris, styling in his shiny suit, patent leather wing tips, and jet-black glasses, resurrected Robert Johnson's "Crossroads" with a harp solo as hot as the hellfire its author accepted as an even swap for his very own soul.

The morning of the second day, I finally made my way to the palace of the King. I'm still not sure what I was expecting to find—a vision of Elvis's spirit, some sense of his continued presence—but Graceland, I'm sad to say, is a haunted house. When I walked in the front door, led along with all the other sheep in my herd, it was as if time had stopped the day Elvis died back in '77. Speaking strictly in terms of interior decoration, what an untimely death. Everywhere there was shag carpet, on all the floors and some of the walls, with sofas and armchairs worthy of the USS *Enterprise*. His mother Gladys's purple bedroom and bath were every bit as rococo as his daddy Vernon's office out back in the shed was militarily minimalist. The coup de grace was a room tackier than anything my mama could have dreamed up, every surface covered top to bottom in wild animal skins. What we were not shown was perhaps as telling as anything on display: the television Elvis executed with his pistol, and the bathroom where he finally gave up the ghost. The spirit of Elvis, it seemed, had left the building. The air felt so depressive by the time my tour group shuffled out the back door into a fine mist of rain, I was grateful to view the gravesite. There he lay, beneath a bronze slab between Gladys and Vernon, beside a fountain just down from the swimming pool. I stood in the drizzle for a while, impressed less by the wreaths, posters, and teddy bears than by the endless and surprisingly international stream of mourners and gawkers.

The only redeeming factor at Graceland was the Elvis Presley Automobile Museum, an impressive brick labyrinth with a '59 aquamarine Cadillac lying like a lion out front and a bevy of classics inside, the most delectable of which, for my taste, was yet another Cadillac, built the year I was born, bright pink from the point of its hood to the tip of its trunk. There were rare Harley-Davidsons and two hog-engined tricycles painted in '70s psychedelia, like something Barbarella and Buck Rogers might have ridden across the face of Mars. In the center of the building stood a white picket fence around rows of old car seats. Up front, a drive-in theater screen showed a loop of movie clips in which Elvis and the Hollywood beauty-of-the-week pretended to ride around in race cars, hot rods, and motorcycles. On the way out I strolled down a glass-lined hallway tantamount to a time machine, where Elvis's outfits from the 1950s, baggy chinos and loose cotton shirts, gave way to the army uniforms and leather of the '60s, and then the regal gaudiness of his '70s-era pantsuits. Somehow it all left a bad taste in my mouth, and I went away feeling not only divinely uninspired but downright cheated and cheapened.

Before leaving Memphis, I sat on the bike and studied my dog-eared map, pondering whether to return home on the interstate through Nashville and Knoxville or ride the narrow roads down to Tupelo to visit Elvis's birthplace. The morning had turned sunny and muggy, with high pillowy clouds offering brief moments of cool breeze. The Weather Channel had warned that a high-pressure system was due to blow through toward evening, but I figured I could make it to Tupelo and be back in Nashville, via the scenic Natchez Trace Parkway, by nightfall. What finally swayed me was the memory of Junior James assuring me it was an unpardonable sin to get that close to Jerry Lee Lewis's house and not go there. So I headed south out of Memphis across the state line into Mississippi.

On a curvy stretch of asphalt near the tiny crossroads called Hernandez, I found the small spread belonging to Jerry Lee, the rocker known affectionately, if not ironically, as the Killer. There was no historical marker, no sign of any kind, but I knew it had to be his place when I spied a one-hundred-yard-long clapboard fence spray-painted from one end to the other with all manner of graffiti, standing along the roadside like some long-lost expressionist painting. The only scrawled comment I can recall was something about "Jerry Lee's lovechild," a wisecrack that cuts close to home. In 1955 my daddy's sister Betty Jean had named her son Jerry Lee before he was stillborn. I came into the world a month later, and Aunt Bet tried her best to talk Mom into giving me the name of her dead child. Unwilling to flirt with the fates, Mom compromised and dubbed me Larry Dean, so I have always felt a kind of spiritual bond with Mr. Lewis, the only man I've ever seen whose hair is wavier than mine.

I pulled into the gravel driveway and was surprised to see a perfectly normal, medium-sized brick ranch house. There was a black Jaguar parked by the side stoop, a large pond in the backyard, and off to the left a ways a corrugated aluminum shed with "THE KILLER'S KAR KOLLECTION" hand-painted above the double doors. (Given Jerry Lee's redneck roots, one wonders if the initials might be intentional.) No sooner had I shut off the bike than a pack of barking dogs ran out from behind the house. I held them at bay with a boot while wrestling my helmet off, and an old man in blue jeans and a T-shirt stepped off the back porch to glare at me as if to say, "What the hell are you doing here?" I wasn't exactly sure myself, so I waved at him and just stood there trying to keep the smallest dog, some kind of fuzzy poodle-mix yapper, from nipping my leg. Finally a casually dressed young woman stuck her head out the side door and called across the yard, "What can we do for you?"

I smiled my relief. "I thought I might take the tour."

"Why, sure," she said. "Come on in the house."

After the crowded, noisy, three-ring circus of Six Flags Over Elvis, it turned out I was the only person here to see the home of the rocker who, in the mid- to late '50s, was giving Elvis a run for his money as the King of Rock 'n' Roll, that is, until he up and married his cousin. I stifled a giggle when the tour guide told me in passing that she was Jerry Lee's first cousin twice-removed, or some such distant kin. The small foyer had been turned into a gift shop, full of the same kind of kitsch I had seen in Graceland's full-blown souvenir store, minus the high prices. My guide spoke with genuine warmth of Jerry Lee's hard life, the loss of two wives and a son, as well as of his generosity in supporting several charitable causes. She failed to mention that at least one of his wives had died under suspicious circumstances.

The house held more pianos than I've ever seen in one place, most of them miniatures donated by adoring fans. The one piano that caught my eye was a hard-worn old upright, its dark wood scarred and the ivory of several keys chipped off. Among all the tacky glamour, this relic leaned against the wall like a poor relation at a family reunion.

"What's that?" I couldn't help but ask.

"Oh, that's the piano Jerry Lee's daddy mortgaged their house to buy when he was just a little thing. He'd drive Jerry Lee and his cousins, Jimmy Swaggart and Mickey Gilley, around the neighborhoods in Farraday, Louisiana, so they could play for nickels and dimes."

Nickels and dimes indeed, I thought as she led me down a long hallway hung from one end to the other with gold records and the many awards Jerry Lee has received over the years. At the end of the hall she pointed to a pair of closed doors leading off to the right. "That's the part of the house where Jerry Lee lives."

"I don't suppose he's home, by any chance."

"No," she said with a proud smile. "He's off touring, but here, take a look at the kitchen."

It was nothing short of a Dr. Seuss moment when we stepped outside and walked around the black-tiled swimming pool cut in the shape of a grand piano, complete with white and black keys at the shallow end. She would not let me linger, however, perhaps because this was where Jerry Lee's young son had drowned. As we stepped back into the gift shop, the TV/VCR showed a ghostly pale wild man, reddish hair as thick and wavy as ever, pounding a life-size baby grand onstage before a stadium chock full of screaming fans. "Oh," she said when she noticed me watching, "there he is in Hungary. After the Wall came down, he was the first Western performer who got asked to play." Now in his sixties, with a past that would have (and has) finished off many a weaker man, Jerry Lee was assaulting the keyboard as if it had insulted his mother's memory. One thing about the Killer: he is a survivor.

On the way to Tupelo my good luck ran out. The chubby cumulus clouds that had moved across the land like grazing elephants now gathered themselves into a thundering herd. The landscape grew dark as twilight, and goosebumps crawled along my forearms and the back of my neck. I slowed my pace to keep one eye on the road and the other on the horizon, praying for a ray of sunlight to announce the far side of the passing front, but the farther I peered into the distance, the darker things looked, like a slowly sinking ceiling of cold gray steel. By the time I reached the house where the King was born, which had just closed down for the day, a thin mist was coating the grass in the little box of a front yard.

I was shocked to see how tiny the house is, really just a shotgun shack, fixed up nicely but small enough to fit into Graceland, which is not that large a mansion, three or four times over. In the parking lot I talked with a man from Missouri, on vacation with his wife and painfully bored teenager. We spoke of Elvis, his classic American rags-to-riches story, and how he had managed to transcend his own background to reach some level of universal recognition. Then somehow we got off on Civil War battle sites, and I felt a sense of brotherhood with this stranger, this Yankee whose forebears kicked the asses of my ancestors in fields and forests not that far from where we stood, a bond forged in our common interest in a man from Tupelo, Mississippi.

When the mist thickened and daylight drooped, I made my way to a restaurant for supper and asked the manager to switch one of the televisions in the bar to the Weather Channel. Sure enough, there was the front, big and green and ugly, barreling toward me from the west. Judging from the satellite maps, I thought I could just make it to Nashville before the bottom dropped out. I was wrong, and not only about the timing. What I didn't realize until too late is that the Natchez Trace Parkway is much like North Carolina's Blue Ridge Parkway, a stunningly beautiful drive in part because there are only a few scattered houses and almost no service stations alongside. As I slipped back into the rainsuit and left the restaurant, Bob Dylan's rasping howl rose up like a dirge in my head:

> One more cup of coffee for the road
> One more cup of coffee before I go
> To the valley below

I ran into a steady rain within the first thirty miles, just far enough out of town to make it a pain to go back, but not nearly far enough to feel committed to the ride through wet and dark. But I pushed on, steering with my hands rather than leaning into the curves to keep the bike from slipping out from under me, praying I would not run over a stray hubcap or board or stone on the roadway. And as full darkness fell, I realized I was getting low on gas.

There is no fuel gauge on bikes like mine, so I was keeping tabs on the mileage. Less than fifty miles out of Tupelo, the bike sputtered as it does when the main tank runs out, so I switched over to the reserve, knowing it held no more than twenty miles' worth of fuel. I searched desperately at every crossover for a filling station, but found nothing, open or closed. There was not nearly enough gas to get back to Tupelo, so I had to push on. Then the first lightning bolt came down like a decree from on high, and my heart went black as the night around me. The rain became one solid mass of water, so when the next flash illuminated a sign for an upcoming intersection, I took the exit. Pulling up underneath the overpass, I parked the bike as far from the road as I could without miring in red mud, fished the flashlight out of my saddlebag, and searched the nether regions of the bridge for any trolls who might be lurking there. It did not help my nerves that I'm an arachnophobe from way back. When I pulled the pack of cigarettes from my rainsuit pocket for a smoke, water and tobacco mush poured out.

So I dug in the saddlebag for a dry pack and sat for a miserable hour through a harrowing thunderstorm, feeling just how far away from home I was, as if the very gods had conspired to prove to me once and for all how foolhardy I can be. Facing sustained danger on the road wears a body down, and then for the fear to rise to a whole new level is more than most of us can bear. Throughout that long hour I sat wet, bone-tired, face-to-face with my own mortality. Many's the sober thought that passed through my head as the sky burst wide open with thunder and lightning. The faces of my heroes, most of them dead and gone long before their time, came to me, and I was strangely saddened to realize I can no longer die tragically young.

But once the storm spent its rage and began to ease, and a longer space of relative quiet stretched out be-tween each lightning bolt and thunderclap, an odd thing happened. My senses came alive. The night took on a fresh aura, and the slackening rainfall dropping from the sky, dripping from the bridge, and flowing down the embankment felt warmer and somehow less threatening. The wind in the trees hushed to a gentle breeze. While moments before it had whipped my hair across my face and stung my tired eyes, it now seemed quite literally to lift my spirits. The very asphalt of the roadway emerging from beneath an inch of rustling water shone with a sparkling light, refracting the beams of a nearby yard light into a quivering nightscape. When the frogs cranked up their Tibetan monk chant in the trees all around, I knew I was going to be all right. There's nothing quite like a taste of vulnerability to make you feel how alive you are at this very place, in this one moment.

When I knew the worst of the storm was gone, I rechecked my map, found the nearest town off the Parkway, and, willing the gasoline to hold out like Elijah's miraculous lamp oil, headed out into the damp night. My first sight of civilization was, of all things, a bingo parlor. When I walked in, the gaping eyes of the locals told me more than any mirror just how rough I must have looked. But one of the men playing cards at a table off to the side, as friendly as he was burly, told me where to find the nearest motel. The bike must have been running on fumes when I got there, but I've never been happier to see a Days Inn sign in all my life.

For two days and three nights I sat in that godforsaken motel room in the corner where Mississippi, Tennessee, and Alabama meet, just me and my cigarettes and the Weather Channel, waiting for the front, which had sat down on me like some stubborn, overworked mule, to pass on into the Gulf of Mexico. Next day, when I ran through the rain to the office and asked the clerk where I could find a beer, she smiled. "Boy, you're in a dry county, but you're welcome to ride over into 'Bama if you want." As a friend put it after I returned home, "There's no such thing as a dry county in Mississippi. You were just asking the wrong people." On the third day, speckles of sunshine peeking through the dark clouds, I said to the clerk as I paid my bill, "Come hell or high water, I'm out of here."

Feeling like Jonah who was swallowed by the whale because he refused God's command to go to Nineveh, I rode back to Memphis for one last stop before heading home. Throughout this long ride, I'd thought I was headed for Graceland, to see Elvis, to walk in the footsteps of the King. How could I have known that along the way I would stumble into the presence of a very different kind of royalty?

In a timeworn, down-at-the-heels section of Memphis, the Civil Rights Museum is built around the Lorraine Motel, where Martin Luther King was assassinated. Across the open courtyard is the balcony where, in the old black-and-white press photo, Dr. King stands with his brothers-in-arms. The picture snapped moments later shows the good Doctor lying where the lethal bullet left him, Jesse Jackson and the others leaning over his body and pointing desperately toward where the bullets were fired. As these stark images rose up from my memory, I felt an inexplicable quivering deep down in the gut. I looked up from the plaque commemorating Dr. King's life just as someone standing behind the plate-glass window of his room happened to be pointing in the same direction. U2's lyric jumped to mind:

> Early morning, April 4,
> Shot rings out in a Memphis sky,
> Free at last, they took your life,
> They could not take your pride.

Standing in patchy sunlight, I swapped stories with an elderly gentleman about the days of our youth, his in Alabama, mine in South Carolina. As it turned out, each of us had suffered assaults for hanging out with friends of the other's race. I told him with shame that in my hometown and even in my own home, where Dr. King's death was prophesied whenever his face appeared on the news, the term "Negro" was preferred over its bastard cousin only in the presence of blacks, and oftentimes not even then. His eyes softened, and he said, "Well, son, all that's behind us now." I wish I could believe it were so.

Surely this man, I thought, *has seen our society change in ways I could never imagine,* yet I stood there sweating in the heat of my ongoing battle against the seeds of racism planted in the innocent soil of my heart before I had ever noticed the difference between white skin and black. When you're told from your mother's knee, verbally and otherwise, "We are better than them," how do you unlearn such a thing? I am sad to say it's a struggle I don't always win, but I will never give up as long as I draw breath. For every stereotype my mind dredges up, I recall the face, the voice, the heart of someone I know who smashes such a preconceived notion.

In stark contrast to the spiritual emptiness of Graceland, Dr. King's ghost haunts the very hallways of the museum, a monument to the legacy of a simple, noble man whose life and tragic death sing out the very spirit of the blues. Its graphic displays chronicle the long, painful history of the civil rights struggle. Alongside a mother and her small children, I sat on a bus where the pasty white mannequin in the driver's seat barked from a disembodied distance, "Go sit in the back, boy!" Wandering onward, we watched film footage of civil rights protesters attacked by police dogs and water hoses. Down a trash-strewn alleyway, stony statues of National Guard troops trained bayonets on a line of garbage collectors carrying placards that read, heartbreaking as it was to be said so simply, and to even need saying, "I AM A MAN." A Ku Klux Klan robe hung from a nail around the corner from the charred carcass of one of the doomed Freedom Rider buses.

Up to this point I had considered myself a spectator, uncomfortable to be such a small minority among these fellow pilgrims whose history is portrayed, mourned, and celebrated here. But the moment I pressed a button and heard the strong voice of Dr. King giving his "I Have a Dream" speech beneath the seated, silent figure of Abraham Lincoln, I knelt down on one knee and wept.

Two elderly women stood nearby and watched what had to be a strange sight, this leathered white biker falling to pieces, and I must confess I felt like an interloper there. But I pulled myself together and stood, knowing that I too have a place in Dr. King's promised land: the civil rights struggle was and is as much to free me as anybody. That's why, as Ben Harper sings his name, "Martin Rod-ney Lu-ther King" means so much to me now that I settle into my fifties, a decade he never lived to see. His dream is a prophetic vision for everyone, that someday we might do unto all others as we would have them do unto us, allowing each one the dignity and respect that comes with being a living creature on this good Earth.

I sat for a while in the courtyard and watched other pilgrims make their way through Dr. King's room, #306, where the bed is still unmade as if he had just stepped out onto the balcony. A tune slipped into my head, mournful and sweet:

> Has anybody here seen my old friend Martin?
> Can you tell me where he's gone?
> He freed a lot of people,
> But it seems the good die young.
> I looked around, and he was gone.

My soul felt every bit as empty as that balcony, and I caught a stark glimpse of the dark profundity of the blues. That was when a little boy, no more than three or four years old, poked his head in the window, and he waved at me. I smiled and waved back. No casual kindness on the part of a stranger has ever made me happier. When a mockingbird hopped nervously across the hot bricks of the courtyard, I stood and headed for the bike and my long journey home, stepping ever so lightly on that hallowed ground so as not to frighten her.

CHAPTER SEVEN

The Valley of the Shadow of Death

I
t is no accident that auto racing, arguably the most dangerous of all major sports, is deeply entwined with religion. Sports such as football and hockey are brutal in their very design, hobbling players with life-affecting injuries and even in some cases partial or full paralysis. Likewise, basketball, once touted as a noncontact sport, takes its toll on players' bodies. But in no other brand of competition are the stakes so high as in racing. Serious harm and even death lurk around every curve.

Add to this the fact that stock car racing was born and bred in America's Southern hotbed of conservative religion, and it should come as no surprise that this sport is so deeply baptized in spiritual waters. David Smale, communications director for Fellowship of Christian Athletes, draws the connection between faith and racing. "A lot of the culture of NASCAR is Southern—the Bible belt," he says. "A lot of people grew up around racing. They also grew up going to church on Sundays, and that's definitely part of the tradition of the culture."[1] As

---

[1] "Holding on Tight," cnnsi.com, October 3, 2001, http://sportsillustrated.cnn.com/motorsports/nascar_plus/news/2001/10/03/fai th_feature_ap/ (accessed January 29, 2007).

my brother likes to put it, "Praise the Lord and pass the guy in front of you."

William J. Baker, professor of history at the University of Maine and an expert on religion and sports in America, draws parallels between the worldviews of athletes and the particular brand of religion most obvious in American sports. "In many ways, evangelical Christianity and big-time sport are similar. Both are win-lose mentalities. In evangelical Christianity you are either saved or lost. You've gone to Heaven or you've gone to Hell. You win or you lose, and that's what sport is all about."[2] As they say in the male-dominated sporting world, "A tie is like kissing your sister." Both subcultures involve black-and-white worldviews where there is no middle ground, no purgatory with the possibility of parole.

Yet such a cut-and-dried dualism between win or lose, saved or lost, brings with it a deep and troubling dilemma, what has been called the problem of evil. If God's in his heaven and all's right with the world, the best man should always win, the good should be rewarded, and the evil punished. End of story. But in sport as in life, sometimes the underdog steals the show. And in life as in sport, all too often bad things happen to good people. The biblical Preacher of Ecclesiastes, who addressed as well as anyone the problem of evil, states, "I

[2] Robert Lipsyte, "Auto Racing: The Crossing of Faith and Big-Time Sport," nytimes.com, March 4, 2001, http://select.nytimes.com/search/restricted/article?res = F50F12F63E5F0C778CDD AA0894D9404482 (accessed February 4, 2007).

returned, and saw under the sun that the race is not to the swift, nor the battle to the strong, neither yet bread to the wise, nor yet riches to men of understanding, nor yet favour to men of skill; but time and chance happeneth to them all" (9:11).

Nowhere is this problem thornier than in the sport of big league racing, in which a split-second failure, a maneuver off by inches, can bring about not only the loss of a contest and its passel of prize money but also the loss of life. And at no time in recent memory has racing, or any other major American sport, confronted its athletes and fans with a more difficult challenge than the death of Dale Earnhardt. Earnhardt's longtime competitor Mark Martin said, "I think Dale Earnhardt's accident had a huge impact on drivers personally. Obviously, it had a huge impact on the fans."[3]

How is it that this small-town high school dropout, a redneck Southern good ol' boy, can embody the most difficult and perhaps the most crucial of all theological problems? Earnhardt was by no means an openly religious man, and tales from the wilder days of his youth still make for juicy gossip in and around his hometown of Kannapolis, North Carolina. Nevertheless, like many a prodigal son he mellowed with age. In his later years he attended a little Lutheran church when he could spend time at home, and during the season he often

---

[3] Tim Tuttle, "Lasting Legacy," sportsillustrated.cnn.com, February 16, 2006, http://sportsillustrated.cnn.com/2006/writers/tim_tuttle/02/16/inside.nascar /index.html (accessed February 4, 2007).

showed up at the infield chapel service on the morning of a race. By all outward appearances he was a man blessed by God, handsome, talented, and self-assured.

In fact, it was precisely because he had about him an air of invincibility that Earnhardt's sudden death struck at the heart of racing's faith in triumph even in the midst of tragedy. "The fact he got killed shocked everybody," said Leo Mehl, international head of Goodyear's racing department. "We all watched racing accidents with Dale and he would walk away. He seemed invincible. He wasn't."[4] This man's demise shook the world of racing to its core and sent ripples all through American society. Why? Because Earnhardt was, like Job in olden times, a righteous man who loved his family and excelled at what he did. How could such an evil thing happen to such a good person?

That soul-searching question lies just beneath the surface of so much that has been said about Earnhardt's death at the age of forty-nine, a time in his life when he was just beginning to settle into the rewards of all his hard labor. Yet I have neither read nor heard an adequate answer. No wonder. The problem of evil is a tough puzzle addressed by all the major religions, and not one of them can offer a fully satisfying solution.

Western religions like Christianity sidestep the issue by claiming that there really is no problem because the unpleasant situation in which we find ourselves is only temporary. In the beginning God created the heavens

---

[4] Ibid.

and the Earth as a place of perfection, and it was Adam and Eve who caused this mess. As Saint Paul says, "The wages of sin is death" (Rom. 6:23), so when things go wrong, according to the dominant Christian view, we get what we deserve. And even if we don't, God will straighten it all out at the Last Judgment, that great reckoning when, as Jesus proclaimed, the last shall be first and the first shall be last.

Religious folk involved in stock car racing, a sport that in many ways, like the recent resurgence of traditional Southern culture itself, reenacts Jesus' rise from obscurity to grab victory from the very clutches of defeat, have adopted this typically Western approach to the problem of evil. Professor Baker parallels the drama of racing and the Christian vision of death and resurrection. "When good old boys say Dale's in a better place now, they mean it. You go to Heaven because you believe in Jesus, not by your good works. You can live your life like a dog, but be saved at the end. And that's like sport, too. You can win on the last lap."[5] Yes, evil is a problem, but only for a while, since we have hope of better things to come.

Furthermore, Eastern religions like Hinduism and Buddhism seek to transcend the problem of evil by claiming that everything in our lives, both good and bad, is the result of karma—that is, what goes around comes around. Our good deeds bring us good, our evil actions bring us evil. According to the Hindu scriptures, "As a

---

[5] Lipsyte, "Auto Racing."

man acts, so does he become. . . . A man becomes pure through pure deeds, impure through impure deeds" (Brihadaranyaka Upanishad). And if in this life our rewards or punishment do not appear to fit the virtue or the crime, the imbalance is due to good or evil deeds done in a previous lifetime before this particular incarnation. Life may seem unfair, but in the great karmic scheme of things everything will level out.

In both Western and Eastern views we find both a lack of hard evidence that ultimately life makes sense, coupled with an appeal to mystery: things may look out of whack in this life, but there is a larger plan than we can see, and we must trust that in the end the books will be balanced. It all comes down to faith—or the lack thereof. Perhaps, then, there is no adequate reply to this nagging question, just as the solutions offered by the world's major religions ultimately fail to satisfy the soul torn by unspeakable tragedy, crying out like Jesus himself at his darkest moment to a seemingly empty sky, "My God, my God, why have you forsaken me?" (Matt. 27:46). And yet we cling to partial answers while we seek comfort as much as clarity.

Perhaps this lack of a full understanding of the existence of evil is why most of us are so adept at the art of denial. Whenever my students and I discuss the problem of evil in my religion classes, I always make a point of asking, "If you had only these two choices, where would you rather be: sitting at your desk in the World Trade Center writing an email or talking on the phone, when all of a sudden you look up and there's an airliner crashing through your window; or would you rather be a passenger in the airliner with plenty of time to know where you're headed and what awaits you at the end?" Every semester, almost all the students choose sudden and unexpected death in their office over a plane ride that gives them a chance to prepare themselves for their last moment. Why is it that we prefer not to ponder the most inevitable moment of every life? To put the question in my students' jargon, "What's up with *that*?" Each of us knows we are going to die—it's an inescapable fact of life. Yet our youth-obsessed culture spends a great deal of time, energy, and money trying to keep ourselves preoccupied so that we do not ever face it.

No one ever accused stock car drivers of being deep thinkers, but it is obvious that many of them have reflected long and hard on this troubling issue. If you volunteered to face danger and death at breakneck speeds on a weekly basis, I dare say you would, too. Kyle Petty, who has logged his share of miles in the valley of the shadow of death, is well aware of the risks involved in racing and has found ways to deal with them. "What we do is obviously a little more dangerous than the ordinary guy sees his job as being," he says. "Tragic things can happen to anyone at any time. We do everything to prepare the car and all the parts and pieces the best we can. Then we prepare ourselves spiritually."[6]

---

[6] David Bochon, "Fueled by Faith," www.livinglightnews.org, no date, http://www.livinglightnews.org/vpetty.html (accessed February 10, 2007).

Every one of us practices a certain level of denial whenever we crank up the car and move our fragile bodies through space at speeds our not-so-distant ancestors knew, though we have forgotten, are unnatural. What Kyle's father Richard observes about racers and wrecks might just as well be said of any of us: "That's the way the racing mind is made: 'It's going to happen. It's going to happen from time to time. But it's going to happen to somebody else.'"[7] One of the racers' most important gifts is a complex combination of sensitivity to physical danger, which keeps them from driving recklessly, coupled with a certain indifference to the possibility of harm. "You get a guy who drives a race car," Petty said, "he's a little like a hunter who could get shot, but he's never thinking about getting shot."[8] Likewise, longtime racing veteran Mark Martin places the problem in a broader context, one in which we all live and, whether or not we choose to consider it, face danger every day of our lives. "Everything is dangerous. You have to weigh the risk about going to the grocery store. Do you go at night? Or do you go during the day?"[9]

Day or night, every time you drive down the entrance ramp to the freeway, you will accelerate to a speed not

[7] Liz Clarke, "NASCAR Races at God's Speed," www.wash ingtonpost.com, April 22, 2001, http://www.washingtonpost .com/ac2/wp-dyn?pagename = article&node = &contentid = A44 527-2001Apr21 (accessed September 10, 2002; no longer available).

[8] Liz Chandler, "A Surprising Toll: 260 Dead," www.charlotte .com, May 25, 2006, http://www.charlotte.com/mld/charlotte/ sports/motorsports/14667060.htm (accessed February 10, 2007).

[9] Ibid.

that much slower than the ones stock car racers travel on the shorter tracks like Bristol and Martinsville. Some motorists, of course, drive much closer to those speeds than others, but if you have ever been involved in or witnessed an accident on the highway, you've seen the horrors that can happen to any of us in the blink of an eye. Why else would we have more and more laws enforcing the use of seatbelts and the installation of airbags as standard equipment?

All professional drivers know they put themselves in danger's way just by climbing into a race car. Some of them speak of survival in terms of fate. Indy car and NASCAR racer A. J. Foyt puts it bluntly, "I always felt that when your time is up, it's up."[10] Others like Geoff Bodine, who was brought to death's door in a fiery wreck during a truck race at Daytona, trust their skills. "We all know that this can be a deadly sport," he admits, "but it isn't a death sport. We don't go out there with the idea in our head that we're going to get killed today. Nothing like that; it's just the opposite. We go out there with the idea that we're going to win. And if we don't, we're going to try next week."[11] Still others see accidents, or their survival of them, as dumb luck. If you follow racing, you have heard drivers countless times describe a wreck as "just one of them racin' deals." As Kurt Busch has said, "I just race as I know how to race and I believe everything will take care of itself."[12] Richard Petty, refer-

[10] Ibid.

[11] Ibid.

[12] "Holding on Tight."

ring to his grandson Adam who was killed in a race-related wreck in 2000, speaks to a driver's acceptance of fate, explaining that there's no use in pointing a finger at racing. "If he was in an airplane," he insisted, "we wouldn't blame airplanes."[13]

Yet for many involved in the sport, religion offers not so much an explanation of life's pitfalls as a source of comfort for those who suffer them. More specifically, there are those who understand what they are doing as placing themselves in God's hands. Shortly after the death of his father, Dale Earnhardt Jr. spoke of the crisis brought about by a face-to-face encounter with calamity and revealed how he dealt with his personal loss. "You've got to have something to lean on," he said. "You can let things either strengthen you or turn you the other way. I chose to believe even more in the Lord."[14] The focus is not on the evil that occurs, but on the way one deals with it.

The elder Petty described with a homespun automotive metaphor his approach to the problem of evil as it arises in racing: "A lot of the time [God] tests us and tests our faith. It's like he says, 'Here's a flat tire, how you going to fix this thing, guys?'"[15] There is little or no interest in explaining why the problem might exist, only in overcoming the difficulties it presents. You will note here the familiar appeal to a faith whose eyes are, if not

---

[13] Chandler, "A Surprising Toll."

[14] "Holding on Tight."

[15] Ibid.

exactly blind, certainly peering, as Saint Paul put it, "through a glass darkly" (1 Corinthians 13:12).

Indeed Jeff Gordon, one of racing's most popular drivers and an avowedly religious man, makes no bones about viewing his profession through the stained-glass window of religious commitment. "For us," he says, death "is something we have to face. One thing that really helps us face that is our faith. It gives us strength. It allows us *not* to focus on the danger parts of it. It allows us just to stay focused on what our jobs are and what we have to do, which is drive as fast as we can. And I think it also helps comfort our families."[16] While many drivers rely strictly on their own natural talents to get them through the tight spots both on and off the racetrack, some draw their strength from a greater power, the mighty bulwark of the creator and sustainer of all things.

Darrell Waltrip is perhaps the driver who has addressed the problem of evil most forcefully. A personal friend of Earnhardt, Waltrip has sought to place the death of his longtime competitor in the broader context of our national grief over the 9/11 terrorist attacks. "In February and again in September [of 2001]," he has written, "we all realized just how quickly our lives can be changed, or they can even come to an end. In the wink of an eye, we can be out of here. Those of us in racing were impacted by the deaths of several drivers these past few years but, most of all, the death of Dale Earn-

---

[16] Clarke, "NASCAR Races at God's Speed."

hardt."[17] To fellow drivers and race fans alike, Earnhardt's demise was a shocking reminder of the daunting fact that everyone, no matter how invincible we may look or feel, is vulnerable to sudden and unexpected death. By the same token, the fall of the World Trade Towers, those seemingly eternal symbols of the American Dream, and the massive loss of life witnessed by so many brought home to us all a renewed sense of our own mortality. It was as if Death itself were saying, "*You* could have been a passenger on one of those airplanes; *you* might well have been working at one of those office desks."

The panic in the stricken voices and faces of those who ran to escape the tumbling towers, not unlike the shiver of disbelief I felt in myself and sensed in others as it dawned on us that Earnhardt was really gone, revealed a deeper dimension of terror the end of life gains when it comes so unexpectedly. Waltrip's words capture this sense of shock: "Dale Earnhardt's death was viewed by millions, and most thought he would be OK. But it wasn't long before we heard those dreaded words, 'On the last lap of the Daytona 500, we lost Dale Earnhardt.' Now folks," he recalled, drawing the parallel between these two tragic events even more closely, "I've got to tell you, I'll never forget that Sunday in February, but the whole world will never forget that Tuesday in Septem-

---

[17] Darrell Waltrip, "Tragedies in Racing, Life Give Cause for Reflection," foxsports.com, December 24, 2001 (accessed September 10, 2002; no longer available).

ber. Thousands of people went to work that day, just like Dale did. They kissed their wives and their children goodbye, and they left for work. They showed up to do their jobs. Not one of them could have imagined what was going to happen to them that day."[18] Many of us mark out our lives by such stunning events as the attack on Pearl Harbor, the assassination of John F. Kennedy, or the space shuttle *Challenger* explosion. These are moments when we tell each other exactly where we were and what we were doing when we first saw or heard the sad news.

Waltrip was a television commentator for the 2001 Daytona race, and I can still recall his trembling voice as he waited, like the rest of the audience, live or otherwise, for news of Earnhardt's condition. "I watched Dale Earnhardt's car hit that wall, and I watched those planes hit the two World Trade Center buildings. All I could do was pray. All I could do was pray for Dale, and all I could do was pray for those people in those two buildings and on those airplanes."[19] Such is the feeling of helplessness one feels in the face of what Rudolph Otto has called *mysterium tremendum et fascinosum*, a mystery that is both tremendous and yet fascinating, overwhelming but magnetic. You know you are in the presence of such a mystery when every fiber of your being tells you to turn away but you simply cannot make your eyes obey. How many times, after all, have you watched the video replay of the Trade Towers falling?

---

[18] Ibid.
[19] Ibid.

To his credit, Waltrip tries to look the mystery of the problem of evil square in the eye—at least he is willing to admit that evil is indeed a problem—but in the end he takes an all too typical side step: "People are always asking me, 'Where was God in these disasters?' Folks, I can tell you. We serve a loving and merciful God, but he lets us make choices. And it's those choices that make us realize how sick this world would be without God. Bad choices draw us closer to God, whether it's on the track or in our everyday lives. And as Christians, it's our responsibility to share that gospel with everyone we know, everywhere we go. We should hate the sin and love the sinner. If we do that, maybe we can cut down on bad choices."[20] In other words, Waltrip seems to be saying that the existence of evil in this world created by a perfect God is *our* fault. This is the centuries-old argument from original sin, which states that if only Eve had not listened to the slippery serpent, all would be right with the world.

I must say I am more than willing to take the blame for my own personal shortcomings, yet I do not see how humans can be held accountable for natural disasters such as hurricanes, floods, and tornadoes—"the finger of God." Nor does it make sense to single out individual humans to bear the brunt of mass wrongs. We speak much too easily of Hitler killing 6 million Jews, as if he did not have any help, or at least permission, from the SS, the Nazi Party, and the vast majority of the German

---

[20] Ibid.

people themselves, or of Saddam Hussein murdering his own people, as though he were the only person responsible for these widespread acts of cruelty. Humans are far from perfect, but there is awesome, inexplicable evil in the world that simply cannot be laid at our door.

Be that as it may, Waltrip does offer a more helpful approach to our experience of calamity even if, like other racers from an evangelical Christian background, he limits his options to one particular religion. "The point is," he says, "racing has its share of tragedies. Life has its share of tragedies as well. How we handle these tragedies and if we learn and grow from them, that's what's important, and that's the question. We realize that we should live every minute of our lives not asking where God was in these situations, but where am I in my relationship with Him? What kind of choices have I made regarding my relationship with Jesus?"[21] Waltrip sees that hard times come to one and all. There is no escaping life's difficulties. So rather than use our energies attempting to explain evil, he argues, we ought to accept its existence, learn whatever lessons we can, and move on in faith that God will ultimately work things out. Evil is a problem and always will be, but it can also be a teacher if we are willing to learn its hard lessons.

Those racers who speak openly of the support they draw from their religious faith point to two main sources: family—both blood kin and the racing clan—and God. Motor Racing Outreach chaplain Dale Beaver,

---

[21] Ibid.

who keeps his finger on the pulse of drivers' spiritual lives, commented in the aftermath of Dale Earnhardt's death: "Everybody said to me, 'Are you getting a lot of people asking about their eternal destiny?' It really hasn't changed. You realize last year that we lost Adam Petty and Kenny Irwin and then Dale, and people have been much more introspective and done a lot more soul-searching. But what I have seen is more team members being more proactive in making the most out of their re-lationships."[22] The relationships drivers look to for strength and comfort in tough times include first and foremost their nuclear families—spouses, children, and parents—and second the larger racing family bonded by their involvement in and deep commitment to an excit-ing and dangerous sport.

Speaking of his first encounter with death at an early age, Kyle Petty testified both to the fact that it was racing that revealed the stark reality of the problem of evil, and to the impact his family had on him at a moment of terri-ble uncertainty. "I had an uncle, Randy Owens," he re-called, "who was killed at Talladega when I was 14 years old. It was during a pit stop during one of my father's races, and a fuel tank blew up in the pits, and it killed him. I could not fathom how that could happen. I'd never lost anybody. But through my grandmother, and through my mother and our family, that is when my re-

---

[22] Mike Fish, "There to Help," cnnsi.com, February 19, 2001, http://sportsillustrated.cnn.com/motorsports/2001/daytona500/ news/2001/02/19/d eaths_fish/index.html (accessed February 4, 2007).

lationship with Jesus Christ came to fruition." Petty then laid out a deeper lesson he learned once his loved ones had pointed him to the straight and narrow path. "I grew up in a time when it wasn't the coolest thing to be a Christian. And when you're 14 or 15, you want to be cool. But I realized that there was more to life than just being cool and hanging out. There was a relationship that you needed with Jesus Christ, and that gave you eternal life."

Because his family responded by offering the deep comforts of their religious faith, this tragedy, which could well have started young Petty down the wide road to cynicism and a devil-may-care attitude so common among those whose lives have been marred by heartbreak, instead brought him into the Christian fold. "I'm not perfect by any stretch of the imagination," Petty concluded, "but from that day forward that relationship with Jesus Christ has been there, and I've always been able to call on him when times are bad or when times are good. I call on him as much when times are good as when times are bad."[23] Petty's faith helps him negotiate life's twists and turns, neither taking the good for granted nor seeing evil as the ultimate victor.

Jeff Gordon also knows the importance of family. Speaking of his former life with his now ex-wife, Brooke, Gordon said, "We pray and read the Bible every night." For him, family and his faith in God help him keep a hectic, danger-ridden lifestyle in perspective. Gordon is

---

[23] Ibid.

obviously a driven man who has spent almost his entire life chasing the dream of being a race champion. As in so many careers, it would be easy to lose sight of loftier goals in the headlong pursuit of glory and riches. Yet faith and family enable Gordon to keep his priorities in order. "Racing," he has insisted, "is not the most important thing in my life." Even while running for the checkered flag, drivers like Gordon try to keep their eyes on life's ultimate prize. As the Fellowship of Christian Athletes' David Smale has put it, "A Christian is who I am. My job is what I do for a living."[24]

Once again, Kyle Petty points out a way that racers, and others as well, can keep their sense of balance in a fast-paced world if they are sustained by God and family. "God should be your first priority when you get up," he has claimed. "I say a prayer every morning and read the Bible, and that's the last thing we do before we go to bed at night. My family is the next thing that's important to me. They travel with me as much as they can to the races, and when I'm home, I'm home. I'm not taking days off to go fishing, and I'm not off doing stuff. I spend time with my family because that's what's important to me."[25] Strength and perspective can come through keeping in touch daily with a deeper spiritual life and taking time whenever possible to be with those we love.

---

[24] Ibid.

[25] "Through the Good and the Bad," EP News Service, www .thegoodsteward.com, April 1, 2002, http://www.thegoodsteward .com/article.php3?articleID=993 (accessed September 10, 2002; no longer available).

Petty knows that the rewards of such a committed lifestyle can be great, especially when times are tough. As mentioned earlier, Kyle's son Adam, an up-and-coming young star in NASCAR's bright sky and fourth-generation heir apparent to the Petty racing throne, was killed on May 12, 2000, in a wreck during a practice run at New Hampshire Motor Speedway. Many parents might have cried out in anger against the Almighty for allowing such a horrible thing to happen to their child, yet Petty recalled that he and his family did not question God. "I think for us," he has said with touching openness about his family's pain and their struggle to overcome it, "we looked at it differently. We saw that for 19 years Adam had been a blessing to us. And yes, it was a loss for us, but we looked at it as a loss for everyone. Yes, it still hurts, and it's incredibly hard to lose a child. I don't think there is a minute of a day that goes by that we don't hurt and think about it."[26] So many families have self-destructed due to the death of a child. The father and mother come to blame themselves or one another, and both parents and siblings suffer survivor's guilt. So it can be seen as a testament to the power of their faith in God and each other that the Pettys have managed to find light in the depths of life's darkest valley.

Indeed, according to Petty, it is this very blood bond that has enabled him and his loved ones to carry on in the face of their loss. The sprawling, extended family

---

[26] Ibid.

that is NASCAR rushed to offer comfort and support in whatever ways they could, and although grateful for their concern, Petty sought deeper sources of solace. "The only thing that sustained" his family, he said, "was our faith in God. The outpouring from the fans was phenomenal." They "sent tons of books on how to deal with grief. But you know, I don't think we ever opened a book. We went straight back to the Bible and read the Bible, and found our comfort there, and not in what somebody else said. We found it in what Jesus said."[27] Such is the strength of scripture that truths spoken in another tongue in a faraway land many centuries ago can carry more weight than the words of one's own contemporaries.

As he stated above, faith in God has become Petty's first priority, above all else. And second is the covenant of family ties. "Every night before we go to bed," shared Petty, "we gather to say prayers. That's a big part of who and what we are, and how we handled Adam's accident and death. We sat and talked about it, and we discussed how things happen and why. I think one thing that came from Adam's accident was how important family is, and how important the people around you and the people you love are. That grounds you a little bit."[28] Petty and his loved ones, it would seem, have met the age-old problem of evil head-on, and rather than splintering under the weight of their loss, they have managed to

---

[27] Ibid.
[28] Ibid.

band together and move forward in faith that somehow, some way, love conquers all—even death.

It may surprise you to find such strong religious commitment among men who risk their lives on a weekly basis. The old stereotype of outlaw bootleggers outrunning the revenuers rears its ugly head here, and it's tempting to see stock car drivers as daredevils with a death wish. Yet many in the sport cannot conceive of racing without the support and comfort of knowing that whatever happens, to borrow the words of a popular bumper sticker, "God is my co-pilot." Indeed, Kyle Petty testifies to the help he believes anyone, not just racers, can gain from religious faith. "I don't think you can go out there and race, and I really don't think you can go out in everyday life, without having Jesus Christ with you."[29] One might see this statement as a limited view of religion, an ethnocentric assumption that Christianity is the best, if not the one true religion, but Petty is speaking of the particular form of faith he grew up in, perhaps the only religion he, like most Americans, has been exposed to firsthand.

Mark Martin is just as adamant as Petty when it comes to the choice he has made for himself. "Being a Christian, there's so much in the Bible, so many teachings in there about how you should live your life and how you should handle situations," he said. "That's how I answer your question: One of the ways I handle and deal with the fears and anxiety and frustrations that

---

[29] Ibid.

I have is through the teachings of the Bible."[30] Likewise, Jimmy Spencer, who has survived a slew of life-threatening wrecks, attests to the assurance his faith offers as he risks life and limb to chase the checkered flag. "We can do everything we want inside the cars" to make them safer, he said. "But the bottom line is, I believe in God. I believe I'm going to go to heaven. And I believe that every one of us is going to die. And He—*not* you or me—is the only one that knows when that's going to happen."[31] We see here the deeper meaning of faith: not some intellectual assent to certain beliefs but rather a steady reliance on the strength of a higher power.

These drivers are speaking on the basis of their own personal experience, and though we may question their open-mindedness, their heartfelt testimonies reveal both a sense of gratefulness to know for themselves such blessed assurance and a concern that others might share the advantages of a life of faith. Martin has sought to set the record straight about which comes first, the danger or the faith: "I don't think because we risk our lives every day, that's why we're Christians. We're Christians because we want to have eternal life. Whether you're risking your life today or not, I want that. The day I decided that guarantee, I went out and got it."[32] The same

---

[30] Larry Cothren, "Racing's Steady, Consistent and Complex Superstar," www.markmartin.org, March 31, 2003, http://www.markmartin.org/historyofmark.html (accessed February 7, 2007).

[31] Clarke, "NASCAR Races at God's Speed."

[32] Angelique S. Chengelis, "NASCAR: Racers Turn to Religion," www.detnews.com, August 17, 2001, http://www.det

dependence on a higher power that sustains these men in their daily lives also bolsters their courage and eases their minds as they race at breakneck speeds.

Furthermore, race team owner Joe Gibbs sees the very danger of racing as a bond for those who face it together, pulling them closer to each other and to God. "It's like that old statement: 'There are no atheists in a foxhole,'" he said. "When those bombs start going off, few of us say, 'Well, I don't know [about God].'"[33] As I tell my students, whenever they have found themselves in a tight spot, when their car spun out of control on an icy road or when they saw the Trade Towers fall, I guarantee one of two things jumped out of their mouths: "Oh my God!" or "Holy shit!" Either way, whether or not they realized it at the time, they have made a religious statement. What I mean by that is both expressions are an attempt to express the inexpressible, to say what cannot be said in words because they cannot wrap their minds around this fearful thing they have confronted. The problem of evil has gripped them, and so they cry out to God, to the world, to themselves, *How can this be?!*

Perhaps this weekly grappling with danger and death is why NASCAR drivers take part in at least four prayers every race day. The mandatory prerace drivers' meeting always ends with a quiet ritual: a prayer for the

---

news.com/2001/motorsports/0108/17/h01-271717.htm (accessed September 10, 2002; no longer available).

[33] Clarke, "NASCAR Races at God's Speed."

safety of all involved. The meeting is followed by a chapel service that is not mandatory but well attended by drivers, crew members, and their spouses. Remembering those hard days after the deaths of Earnhardt, Adam Petty, and Kenny Irwin, driver Bill Elliott bore witness to the impact of the chapel services on those who attend. "Everything that's happened in the past year and a half," he said, "it helps everyone deal with it."[34] Following the service, everyone makes their way out to the track and, as the crowd revs up for the start of the race, Motor Racing Outreach chaplains pray individually with each driver in those electric moments after they are strapped into their vehicles and before the command to start their engines. Finally, before the green flag drops and the cars rumble into the first turn, drivers, race crews, officials, and fans bow their heads for a public prayer led by a local minister.

"Prayer's a powerful thing," claimed Jeff Gordon, who knows both the dangers of racing as well as the comforts of religious faith. "When you have God in your life, I think it gives you a peace in life-or-death situations."[35] As we have already seen with Kyle Petty, Gordon has spent time thinking about the role death inevitably plays in an inherently dangerous sport. Note again there is no attempt to explain the presence of death in racing, much less in life. Like so many, Gordon accepts our mortality as a necessary part of the way things

[34] Chengelis, "NASCAR."
[35] "Holding on Tight."

are and is thus more interested in what he can do to live and succeed in spite of it. For him faith is a means of focus, a lens through which he can concentrate more clearly on what is really important.

Such faith even gives Gordon and his race team a sense of the right way to go about what they do. "There is a fine line in our sport," he admitted, "between trying to do the right thing and trying to do the competitive thing that puts you over the top to win. We've had a lot of conversations in our Bible studies about that. God wants us to do all of what we know in our abilities to win the race, but we all know in the back of our minds what wins a race in a way that you'll feel proud and what wins a race in a way that you're not very proud of."[36] Courage to face down danger and guidance to do the right thing are two of the assets available to those who choose to live and race with a deeper commitment to spiritual values.

As with the multitudes of race fans and even many as yet unfamiliar with the sport, the death of Dale Earnhardt touched Jeff Gordon, one of his fiercest competitors. "Of all the people that have had serious injuries or have died," he recalled, "I probably knew Dale the best. I wasn't very close to Adam Petty, and I knew Kenny Irwin but I wasn't very close to him." Perhaps the depth of the impact of Earnhardt's death shows most tellingly in how understated Gordon was when speaking of it. "Certainly, with a guy like that, when something like

---

[36] Lipsyte, "Auto Racing."

that happens, it hits very close to home."[37] In the silence of a memorial service, as the organ plays its sad, mournful tune, there is time and space to think not just of the one who is gone but also of our own mortality, the inescapable fact that someday, sooner or later, our time will come.

Before I was old enough to attend funerals, whenever someone in my family died, it always seemed as if they had simply disappeared. When I was five years old, my dad's father, Papaw Russell, quite literally passed away. One day he was there, playing with us in the dusty front yard, and then he was just gone. I never saw him again. Such is the finality of death, and no amount of remembrances, no late-night wakes, no tears or howls of grief can lessen its painful mystery. Saint Paul's cry still echoes through the ages, "O who shall deliver me from the body of this death?" (Romans 7:24), as do the Buddha's last words, "Have I not already told you that it is in the very nature of all things near and dear to us that we must divide ourselves from them? How is it possible that whatever has been born should not perish?"[38]

Contemplating the possibility of his own death in a racing accident, Gordon has pointed to an even greater reward than courage and guidance. "I think people that know me—maybe as sad as they may be—I think they'd also be very comforted, knowing that I was strong in my

---

[37] Dave Caldwell, "A Talk with Jeff Gordon," BeliefNet.com no date, http://www.beliefnet.com/story/85/story_8557_1.html (accessed January 30, 2007).

[38] Mahaparinibbana Sutta, Digha Nikaya, 2.99f, 155–56.

faith and knowing that I'm in a better place. And I'm probably actually happy and smiling."[39] Who in their right mind would dare race against a man unafraid of his own death? And yet this is the allure of high-speed racing. If my hero is brave enough to take the ultimate risk, then I too can have the strength to go on in the face of life's everyday dangers.

In an interview not long after the elder Earnhardt's death, Dale Jr. was asked by Darrell Waltrip, "You believe your dad went to heaven?" Like Gordon, Junior responded with an affirmation of that "better place" awaiting the righteous after death: "I'm pretty sure of it, actually. He was pretty adamant about living right and being right. He was pretty strong about all that. It's easy for me to say this and a lot of people probably won't take it as seriously coming from his son, but he was fascinating. He was a special person. There [were] just things that he could think of and do, and his level of common sense was so far beyond a lot of people that I know. I just believe he was so way above average in a lot of areas, and that's why I feel pretty positive that he's in heaven because I don't think God would pass something like that up."[40] This young man shows no pretense at a sophisticated theology, and here is not the place to go into the long-standing debate among Christians over faith versus works. It is enough for Junior that his father was

[39] Clarke, "NASCAR Races at God's Speed."

[40] "Heavenly Father," allwaltrip.com, April 6, 2001, http://msn.foxsports.com/other/story/7853 (accessed January 30, 2007).

a good man, and though his life was cut short on that fateful day at Daytona, surely God will reward the righteous. Life on Earth may seem at times a dark and dreary vale of tears racked by inexplicable evil, but those who expect a balancing of the books in the life to come can overcome adversity.

Religious or not, as my younger brother likes to say, every driver snacks on danger and dines on death, and race fans feed off such an adventurous attitude. Precisely how these athletes control their fear of physical vulnerability and handle the weight of their own mortality is perhaps a matter for the psychologists to decide. Nevertheless, for a righteous remnant of racers God is motivator, guide, and goal.

Dodging momentary harm is a common enough experience, something we all do every day, whether it's keeping balance in a slippery shower, fending off a snapping dog, or swerving to the right when an oncoming car crosses the center line. Yet a crucial component of a racer's athleticism, perhaps the most underrated aspect of the sport, is the intestinal fortitude it takes to drive on the ragged edge, as fast as the car can go without spinning out, for four and five hours at a time. How do the racers keep up their nerve under such strenuous conditions for such an extended period of time? Every driver has found ways of dealing with the stress. Many practice rituals to maintain their focus and avoid fatigue or distractions, and some of these rituals are specifically religious.

Before every race Stevie Waltrip, wife of the now-retired racing veteran Darrell, taped a Bible verse on the dashboard of Dale Earnhardt's car. Darrell recalled that on the day Earnhardt died, Stevie was the last person he spoke to before climbing into his race car. Earnhardt took the verse and gave Stevie a kiss on the cheek. Ironically enough, the verse read, "The name of the Lord is a strong tower; the righteous run into it and are safe" (Proverbs 18:10, RSV). Now on racing day Stevie tapes a verse in the car of Earnhardt's son, Dale Jr.[41]

As hectic as a stock car race can be, there is also a good deal of downtime when the drivers must slow to follow the pace car during caution laps and occasionally stop altogether if a race is red flagged because of rain. Jeff Gordon, who also keeps a Bible verse taped to the dashboard of his race car, pointed out there are times to contemplate the scriptures and times to keep your eyes on the road. When the race has slowed, he said, "I'll look at it, read it, and I'll do a little prayer here and there if I feel the need to."[42] These off moments might well be the toughest of all to endure, since the racer's senses are freed from intense concentration on race traffic, hair's breadth drafting, and dodging wrecks. At rest in the

---

[41] Theresia Whitfield, "A Driven Heart," sportsspectrum.com, no date, http://www.sportsspectrum.com/articles/article3.html (accessed February 4, 2007).

[42] Dave Caldwell, "Godspeed," Beliefnet.com, August 2001, http://beliefnet.com/story/85/story_8550_1.html (accessed January 30, 2007).

midst of danger, the mind can be pulled into deep and sometimes dark waters.

As you may know from your own experience of high-speed, often competitive driving in heavy freeway traffic, a part of the brain never stops wandering. There is a stream of consciousness that flows on no matter how preoccupied with the road we may be. In fact, as I alluded to earlier, the very act of piloting a vehicle for an extended period of time might be as close to meditation as many Americans ever experience. I speak here of a long-standing tradition of active meditation rather than the more popular passive form of sitting quietly, doing nothing. Untold generations of Hindus and Buddhists, among others, attest to the life-changing effects of such practice.

Whenever I see a race-car driver overcome with feelings in the winner's circle, as high as a kite on pure adrenaline and grateful right down to his bones to have confronted and conquered death, I wonder if he hasn't at some level enjoyed a religious experience, both physical and spiritual, of the most common kind.

Surely much of the appeal of racing, aside from all the flash and noise and our cultural fixation on fame and riches, is this very experience of transcendence. Getting caught up in the excitement of a race draws us up and out of our everyday world for a while and, because we so often seek to live our lives through the exploits of our heroes, teases us with a taste of vicarious victory. So for a few hours on a Sunday afternoon we can find strength to survive the little deaths that come to us whenever we endure disappointments, suffer sickness, and bear up under boredom, as well as a measure of comfort and assurance while we await our own passage through the valley of the shadow. In the final analysis, racing can be seen at its deepest level as a morality tale acting out ultimate triumph even in the face of defeat and offering living examples of courage, what Ernest Hemingway described as guts: grace under pressure.

CHAPTER EIGHT

The Long Ride Home

The baking blacktop shimmered in the distance like the waving water of a mirage, as if the highway led right down into an ever-receding sea. Ol' Blue's tired fan did its best to keep my feet from melting, and after rolling down the windows and opening the side vents, I put on my Gamecocks hat to keep the hair out of my eyes. Still, the truck was a rolling hotbox, seat and jeans glued to thighs and buttocks by a thickening layer of sweat. That, dear reader, is traveling old school through the dog days of summer.

What is it that occupies your mind in all those long road miles between here and there? My thoughts drifted through well-worn worries brought by the love of my life who, in ways she neither understands nor is able to avoid, simultaneously pulls me toward her even as she pushes me away. For my own part I am apparently all too willing to join in this tragic two-step, all the while adding a few fancy, frustrating steps of my own. It takes two to tangle.

Deeper still but in so many ways related, I sensed beyond the trees and billboards whipping past my window some hidden, more dangerous destination to this psychological safari, a heart of darkness as yet unrevealed and as intimately intertwined with my soul as birth itself. I had set out for Mooresville, North Carolina, a two-and-a-half-hour drive from home, to visit what has long stood in my mind as a holy shrine: the headquarters of Dale Earnhardt Inc. Like a medieval pilgrim trudging across the low hills of France toward some massive stone cathedral in hopes of glimpsing a relic of her patron saint, the skull of Saint John the Baptist, an arm bone of Saint Peter, or, most prized of all, a sliver of the True Cross on which Jesus himself was crucified, I felt a driving need to go see for myself this monument built and named for my hero and, perhaps, to walk where his own feet had once trod.

What exactly I hoped to gain from a trip that felt at times like a fool's errand, I cannot rightly say. One thing I can assure you that I neither hoped nor managed to find was closure, because quite simply closure does not exist. Not in this world, at least. The nature of loss is just that: a gap, a void, a ragged tear in body and soul. The best we can hope for is a not-so-nasty-looking scar. Although religious faith may offer some comfort, complete closure comes only to those who need consolation more than they require truth. Deep pain eventually eases through the cold, slow mercies of time passing. We hide our hurts deep inside flesh and bone, in the inner sanctum of our heart of hearts, and the last pangs of muscle memory cease only when we do, if then.

And so it was that I pulled into the DEI parking lot not really knowing what to expect. For one thing, the place is not so easy to find, set down in the middle of nowhere off a country road winding through horse pastures and farmland. You would think a corporation of this magnitude could afford to put up a few road signs to aid any and all seekers, but there were few to be found. However, once you're on the right route—North Carolina has christened this stretch State Highway 3 in honor of its favorite son—as they say, you can't miss it. The complex is rather large as racing garages go. Two enormous brick buildings face the road, the façade of the headquarters proper an arc of shiny metal and mirrored glass.

I have to wonder if, when Earnhardt's pal Darrell Waltrip dubbed DEI's fancy digs the "Garage Mahal," he was aware that the original Taj Mahal was built as a memorial to love and loss, erected by a seventeenth-century Indian king to honor the memory of his beloved queen, lost in childbirth. Which is not to say that these fancy facilities are the eighth wonder of the world, but rather an impressive piece of modern rural architecture, the Jiffy Lube of the Gods, if you will. As much as I admired the aesthetics of the main building's exterior, the air-conditioned indoors was a welcome relief from the humid heat.

Parked just inside the double glass doors is the familiar jet-black GM Goodwrench Chevy Lumina that Dale drove to his seventh and last season championship in 1994. I immediately knelt down not so much in worshipful devotion, though this hunk of steel and rubber certainly had the aura of an icon about it, but rather in order to get a better angle for a photograph. Older cultures erected statues or painted pictures, but "taking" photos has become many contemporary cultures' way of saying, "This object I now record is important and worthy of remembrance. I hereby claim something of its essence to have with me always." I leave it to the experts in such matters to parse out the differences between this form of reverence, if I may use that term, and the acts of adoration that have emerged around more specifically religious artifacts like the statues of Buddha that adorn the temples on Mount Fuji, the ceremonial stone and metal tools wielded by ancient Mayan priests, or—oddest of all—the black meteorite cocooned within the stone shrine that Muslims call the *Kabah*. Such sites spark a similar response within those who visit: a wish to commemorate time spent in this space, as close as one might ever come to standing in the presence of the one whose life and death are honored here.

The next thing I noticed, to my surprise, was how small the area open to the public actually is—perhaps 30 feet deep and 150 feet wide. To the left is a trophy room and to the right the gift shop doing a brisk business. Like a good Hindu taking home a water-smoothed stone from the sacred river Ganges, a memento to remind her of these holy moments, I performed the capitalist ritual of exchanging the specially marked paper imprinted with religious symbols and endowed with value, what we call cash money, for a black ball cap with the magic number 3 emblazoned in red and white above its bill. On the far side of the backdrop behind the championship

Chevy centerpiece, a 25-foot section of wall has been cut away and glassed in to provide a kind of aquarium, only the fish here are rows of high-horsepowered race cars from the DEI stable that have won various trophies for Dale Sr., Junior, and the rest of the team over the years.

The tension of finally finding myself in a place long anticipated was eased by the fact that I was surrounded from the moment I had walked in by God's good people, the salt of the Earth so long scorned by both upper class and intelligentsia, rough-edged, rednecked, outcaste, often uneducated, easy to anger, and almost always underpaid. These humans are, as the students at Elon would say, my peeps, the common folk whose slang was my first language and whose disdain for dilettantes cloistered within the cozy confines of the ivory tower I still share, only from inside the ivied walls rather than out. Whatever else you might think of those locked out of the comforts of college life and forced to pursue more practical trades—arts and crafts like automotive repair, housekeeping, plumbing, or carpentry, and who have therefore been branded the Great Unwashed—it would behoove you to read (or reread) John Steinbeck's great American novel *The Grapes of Wrath*, in which the desperately dirt-poor family's matriarch, Ma Joad, all but whispers with what my mom's mom liked to call fire in her eyes, "'We're the people that live. They can't wipe us out; they can't lick us. We'll go on forever, Pa, 'cause we're the people.'"

I said earlier that I came to this place in hopes of walking in Dale's footsteps. How could I have known the opportunity would present itself in quite literal fashion? One of the displays along the wall on the way to the gift shop was a line of racing shoes, right foot only, not unlike the soft-soled lace-ups worn by boxers. Below each shoe was the name of its wearer, Dale Sr., Dale Jr., and so on, and next to each was the outline of a shoeprint. Of course I could not resist the temptation to step forward and place my own right foot in the outline next to Dale Sr.'s shoe. I was only mildly disappointed, knowing this was somehow as it should be, to find I didn't quite measure up. Smiling at the cheesiness of it all, I walked on with a visual reminder of how tough it must be for Dale Jr., as is true for so many sons and not a few daughters, to fill their father's shoes. For what it's worth, fans of the #8 driver can rest assured that Junior's foot is exactly the same size as his dad's.

Along the entire back wall of the trophy room, oddly reminiscent of the clothing display I had found at Elvis's Graceland shrine, hang tall glass frames encasing some of the fire-retardant suits Dale wore during his twenty-five-year career. Some of them look brand new, several seem well-worn, and the sleeve of one bears the scar of intense battle, a chunk of rubber melted into the seared left sleeve during a fiery crash. A video monitor suspended from the ceiling in the far corner was blaring rock and country music recorded at the inaugural Dale Earnhardt Tribute Concert staged in 2003 at Daytona International Speedway and hosted by Dale's widow, Teresa. A lighted glass case at the center of the room holds twenty or so trophies from races and championships won. The golden-, silver-, and chrome-plated pieces, given pride of place here in this solemn sanctuary, once again brought to mind statues of Buddha, Shiva, and the Virgin Mary found in stupas, temples, and cathedrals around the world.

It was nothing short of painful to stand before a blown-up photograph of Dale, who is squatted down on one knee after having just won another race. Behind him, her hand resting on his shoulder, is Teresa, beaming one of those "this moment should never end" smiles. Dale has wrapped his right arm around the waist of their daughter, Taylor Nicole, who looked to be about ten years old at the time of the shot. The innocence of her preadolescent face, the unknowing, as yet untested confidence of her raised right hand with forefinger extended in celebration of her father's finishing first was just about all the heartbreak I could take, and so I turned to go.

I wonder if anyone has ever been arrested for operating a motor vehicle under the influence of overwhelming emotion. If driving while weeping could be considered a form of impairment, well, for a little while I was downright dangerous. And so I rode slowly along the country road, tall cornstalks glistening through the tears. What brought me back around was the sight of a '57 Chevy 10 pickup just like my very first truck except that this one was royal blue and mine was one part yellow and two parts rust. It's strange what odd objects can bring us comfort. Before I reached the interstate, my heavy heart had eased somewhat and, considering the emotional minefield I had just maneuvered through, the steady

drone of tires on pavement began to bring a sense of certainty that my grieving process had passed an important
milestone.

As it turned out, DEI headquarters was only the first
leg of the daylong trek. The second sacred site on my
itinerary, though only twelve miles away as the crow
flies, stood nonetheless at a daunting distance on the far
side of the dark vale that separates the living from the
dead. The Dale Earnhardt Memorial sits smack in the
middle of Kannapolis, the small Southern town where
Ralph's son came of age as just one more good ol' boy
with a car and a dream. It was late afternoon now, the
hottest part of the day, and by the time I turned off the
interstate and headed toward downtown, my belly was
so empty my ribs were scraping against my backbone.
Here's a little travel tip, free of charge: if you ever want
to party, don't go to Kannapolis. I figured I'd eat supper
first so as not to sit with Dale's death on an empty
stomach, but ended up spending the better part of
an hour driving from one end of town to the other in a
futile search for a restaurant that serves wine with the
evening meal.

The one redeeming moment of this doomed detour
came at a red light while waiting to cross Highway 29,
Kannapolis's main drag. I sat in rapt admiration and
studied the beloved lines of one of my all-time favorite
cars, built the year I was born, a '55 Chevy Impala. This
sad old sedan had seen much better days, its deserted
carcass tossed like a rusty bucket beside a dilapidated
house across the road. It took a car horn from behind to

wake me from my reverie. *One of these days*, I thought as my foot hit the gas and Ol' Blue jumped to life. *One of these days . . .*

Finally forsaking the search for supper and no doubt preoccupied by hunger pangs, I drove up and down the brick streets of Cannon Village, the site where road signs said the memorial could be found, but with no luck. Have you ever tried to find a place you know is near but just won't reveal itself, as if it's slipped into some time/ space warp, concealed in plain sight? Three red-faced stops for directions later, I finally spied the small brick and grass courtyard over the center of which looms a bronze likeness of the Intimidator that looks to be, appropriately enough for a man who was and still is larger than life, ten feet tall.

Not a soul was there. Cars were parked all around but the place felt, to quote Patty Griffin's sad song, "as empty as the inside of me." Stone silence, except for ghostly whispers of distant traffic whipped about by the wind of an approaching thunderstorm. Despite the sly grin, Dale looked lonely standing there with his arms crossed over his heart, left foot cocked to one side as if to say, "Yeah, it's me. I by God raced 'em all, and the only one who could catch me in the end was the Bastard that beats every single one of us sooner or later, no matter how fast or brave or strong." I don't believe I have ever been so sure as I was in that moment of death's hold on life, its inevitability, and its role as the ultimate goal of living rather than an interruption. I squatted down on one knee to take a photo, and if a camera can steal a statue's soul, then I slipped away with a little of Dale's spirit, a touch of his strength, and a ton of sadness.

Slaking Blue's thirst for gasoline at a nearby corner service station, I was told how to get back to I-85. As soon as the young man behind the counter said Lane Street, the real reason for all my rambling was at last revealed. Roads hold memories every bit as surely as songs or smells. This very street, I remembered as I rode along between boxy little mill houses and mostly mowed lawns, would send me not only to the interstate but, if I chose to follow, on out into the country and eventually to the house where Mom had settled with the man who rescued her from floundering not long after she and Dad had parted.

Windy Knoll was what she called the ranch-style home built by her husband for his first wife, who had succumbed to cancer a few years before he met Mom. The orange bricks of the house might well have sprung right up out of the red Carolina clay of what had once been a cornfield, just a stone's throw from the old wooden family homestead long since fallen back into the Earth. And indeed it was a breezy place, at least on the carport where Mom and I would sit and smoke, whenever she had stopped quitting, and watch the humming-birds zoom in to sip sweetened water from the feeders she had hung while the windchimes she so loved tinkled their tiny tunes.

What mortal has ever unraveled the thorny knot that is our relationship with the woman inside of whose belly we lived and moved from the very beginning of our being until the screaming, bloody moment she pushed us out into this less than welcoming world? Why is birth seen as beautiful while death seems unthinkably ugly, especially since we are seldom ever nearer to dying than in the very act of being born? Innocently enough, as each baby enters this life, that child also brings its own mother to death's door. Everything after the clipping of the cord is a separation and a search for independence from our all too human source, and even in the midst of her joy and relief a mother's tears are surely salted with sorrow for having birthed this baby who itself will some-day die.

Though she lived to be seventy, something of a sur-prise to all who knew her, Mom and I never stopped struggling to secure a separate peace. All other avenues exhausted, I had allowed geographical distance to do what I was unable to accomplish. We had seen one an-other less and less toward the end, and yet I had never given up hope that somehow we would find a way through our emotional maze and make amends, or least let by-god's be by-god's, as it were.

All of this rolled through my mind as I sped along beneath darkening clouds past the place where Mom al-most died when her husband had rear-ended another car, tossing my mother, who was both too stubborn and too fidgety to wear a seatbelt, into the windshield and leaving her face black and blue for days afterward. As was her way, she had enjoyed all the drama and later claimed that the walnut-sized knot on her brow had fi-nally knocked some sense into her head. Perhaps, though no one will ever know, this gallows humor was her way to celebrate surviving a suicide attempt back when my brothers and I were little, followed in every decade after by psychosomatic surgeries and medications and therapists. It makes me sad to feel that Mom had never really wanted to walk through a world that is so hard on those who for whatever reason lack the inner armor to fight what the ancient Greeks feared as the Furies, suffered in biblical times as demons, understood in more modern days as psychological problems and even more recently as syndromes.

Where Lane Street intersects the interstate, I was forced to brake behind an eighteen-wheeler slowly lurching its way toward the Waffle House on the far side of the highway. I so wanted to cross over and continue on to Windy Knoll to sit down one last time with my stepfather, if for no other reason than to say thank you once more for taking good care of my dear mother even when she was truly troubled in body and soul. Not that Jim would expect any such thing as gratitude, this tough old goat who had labored forty years in the textile mills of Concord and Kannapolis after walking the streets of devastated Japanese cities with the U.S. Army infantry occupation forces in the dark days following the horrors of Hiroshima and Nagasaki. Like my own father, Jim had loved my mother and gone head-to-head with her stubbornness. What's more, he had shagged with her on the dance floors of Myrtle Beach and taken her countless miles on the back of his huge Honda Gold Wing.

Up ahead the struggling semi had finally found its way into a parking lot, and I paused there at that cross-

road while a drop of sweat slipped slowly down between my shoulders, unsure which way was the real
road home. Maybe what freed me to turn the wheel and
head down the entrance ramp was the sense that all I
could have done, and then some, to make peace with
Mom, in spite of all my many failures I did my best to
do. If time had allowed, no doubt someday we would
once again have sat side by side in her painted rocking
chairs and talked softly of nothing in particular, laughing at the silliness of it all. Be that as it may, the deepest
comfort I will carry with me to my own grave comes
with knowing God or karma or dumb luck or whatever
it was chose to grant her what must surely be the easiest
death anyone could ever ask.

Almost exactly a year ago, Jim woke to find Mom
lying cold and still in the bed beside him. He called his
daughter up to the house from the trailer out back where
she lives with her husband, a member of the local volunteer fire department. Herself a certified emergency medical technician, Debbie assured us all at the funeral that
Mom showed not one sign of struggle or distress. She
and her sister Julie stood watch over Mom's body until
the very end, even arguing a little, as siblings are wont
to do, over how her hair should look as she lay before us
in the funeral home. What word other than grace can do
justice to the fact that, after the hellacious life she had
led, Mom slipped over to the other side in the sweet
peace of sleep surrounded by those who loved her.

We all should be so fortunate.

There was no time for pondering such things because, before I had accelerated enough to merge into the

slow lane, fat drops like God's own tears were slapping against the windshield. The sky turned darker shades of gray until it blacked out altogether near the horizon. Down the road a ways, a jagged lightning bolt slammed down from cloud to ground, blinked on and off like a bulb, and then vanished. Traffic slowed as a solid wall of rain engulfed us all, and soon a thunderclap rattled the windows. Blue's wipers run only one speed, somewhere between slow and intermittent, so I strained my eyes to watch the taillights of the vehicles in front of me. When the rain thickened even more, every car slowed to a crawl. Another bolt, this one much closer than the first, shot out of the sky and looked to have landed in the median not all that far down the road. Several vehicles pulled off into the emergency lane as a rumble of thunder rolled through. My fingers gripped the wheel until the joints ached, eyes staring straight as if to will the other drivers not to make any sudden moves. I almost wet my pants as one last flash and bang came down just over my head.

The storm turned out to be as brief as it was intense, and the rest of the ride home was marred only by growing hunger and fatigue. Too stubborn and fidgety, I suppose, to stop earlier, I pushed on until I was less than an hour from Hillsborough so that I could eat in a familiar restaurant near the campus where I teach. Grateful not to be moving, I found a stool at the bar beside two businessmen talking shop and knocking back Scotch on the rocks. The bartender put down the shot glass she was polishing, walked over, and asked what I'd like to drink. I didn't realize just how tired I was until I heard the sound of my own voice all but whisper, "House char-donnay, please."

That's when I remembered I had not spoken all day. Those who live alone know that such extended silence can leave you not only breathy, as if the lungs have fallen asleep, but even a bit panicked if loneliness begins to bleed through. So when the woman brought the wine, I pushed myself to speak. "I hope you don't mind me asking," I said, "but I'm guessing there's a story behind that scar on your forehead." She did indeed have quite a mark, like an angry pink Z stamped into the flesh of her right temple.

I was glad to see her smile at such an awkward question. "No," she said. "I don't mind you asking, and yes, there's a story. It was a car wreck."

Oh Lord, I thought. *What a way to end this road trip.*

Without hesitating, she launched into a tale no doubt told many a time. "It happened over by Raven Pharmacy. Me and my husband hydroplaned in a nasty thunderstorm. Hit that telephone pole right there on the corner."

Damn, I thought, then asked, "Seatbelt?"

"Oh yeah," she said. "The only thing that saved my life."

"You're lucky to be here."

"Yeah, the good Lord was watchin' over me," she said and turned to pour another highball for one of the men.

To myself I said, *Actually, dear stranger, if the good Lord had been watching over you, the car never would have hydroplaned, or you'd have missed the pole.*

Later, when I stood to go with a full belly and a lot more strength, I caught her eye before heading out into the evening for the last leg of my quest. "Ain't it good to be alive?" I asked.

She matched me smile for smile.

CHAPTER NINE

Death, Be Not Proud

I was already in mourning when I saw the twin Trade Towers fall. My heart's been bruised ever since February 2001, when I lost my hero, Dale Earnhardt. All those thousands of deaths in the 9/11 terrorist attacks took my grief to a level deeper than I could ever have fathomed. God knows that eerie morning unleashed a hell mouth of horror unimaginable even in our wildest dreams, and for days after I downloaded images from the *New York Times*, candid photos of smiling individuals who fell so suddenly and so far into Ground Zero, until I could put a human face on the carnage. But I had to struggle to find a personal connection with those who died there and at the Pentagon and in that grassy field in Pennsylvania. Dale's death was a more intimate loss, wrapped now in a greater tragedy. Grief takes its toll, even as it takes its time.

Since the dark suicidal days of my midtwenties, I've been fascinated by the mysterious moment of death. What's it like in the final second before we leave this mortal coil: awful agony or sweet release? That confession may strike you as weird, even crazy, but I suspect I'm not the only one who ponders the more personal side of our mortality. Why else would you shell out good money to see *Scream* or *Saw* or any number of movies and television shows whose climax is the death of a character with whom you in some way identify? You can call it the cathartic value of drama, but what you're getting, perhaps even seeking, when you watch these actors die is a foretaste of inevitable things to come.

I've had ample opportunity to mull over life's last second these past few years, ever since his last lap when Dale Earnhardt took what's been called "that awful right turn." Then came NASCAR's controversial report on the crash that killed him. The 324-page document dissected in minute, moment-by-moment detail the curious collision of circumstances that snapped the life out of my favorite driver.

Earnhardt was stubborn enough to wear an open-face helmet rather than the supposedly safer full-face version. His shoulder harness, apparently not installed according to the manufacturer's specifications, shredded under the tremendous pressure of impact and allowed his body to fly farther forward than it would have otherwise. But what killed the man was a matter of sheer timing, of being in the wrong place at precisely the wrong time: Earnhardt's race car bumped another on its way to the retaining wall, twisting his torso, head, and helmet to the right and exposing his neck and jaw to the brunt force of the collapsible steering wheel. If that didn't finish him off, the whiplash as his #3 machine rebounded off the concrete barrier certainly did.

The absence of even one of these factors might have meant Earnhardt would be racing the next weekend, bruised but unbowed. The report implies that it was a combination of factors rather than any single element of the crash that sealed his fate. Yet the seatbelt maker, Simpson Performance Products Inc., cried foul against NASCAR and its official report for placing too much blame on the shredded harness. Simpson claimed that if it had been installed properly, the belt would have done what it was supposed to do. This is the kind of disagreement that lawyers salivate over, but one thing was certain from the get-go: the report, which read like it had been gone over with a pricey attorney's fine-tooth comb, was presented to the media as if to a jury. You can bet that in addition to all their justifiable concerns for driver safety, NASCAR took every conceivable step to cover its billion-dollar behind.

The only real surprise in the report on the Earnhardt tragedy was that NASCAR recommended but did not require its drivers to wear what is called the HANS device, a restraint system built to hold the head and shoulders in place during an accident and thus lessen the possibility of impact and whiplash. But the top brass knew how stubborn its foot soldiers can be, and before the crash at Daytona, only a few wore the device. Ironically, Earnhardt never hid his disdain for such "sissy stuff," and it is a measure of how hard his death struck his peers that in a race shortly after the Daytona tragedy, forty-one of the forty-three drivers strapped themselves into the HANS.

If you've ever been involved in a car wreck, you may know that uncanny sense of time decelerating and everything flowing by like a slow-motion instant replay. I can't help wondering what Earnhardt was thinking in those last sad moments. Knowing his penchant for stubborn fearlessness, I suspect it went something like, "Aw hell, here we go again. Another smashed car and unfinished race." Ultimately, there's no way to know his final thoughts, any more than we'll ever figure out who was really responsible for his death: the maker of the shoulder harness, the men who installed it, the sport that sanctions such daredevil antics, or those of us who pay to watch our heroes flirt with death. Anyone who follows racing will tell you Earnhardt walked, limped, or was carried away from much deadlier-looking wrecks, but in the final analysis, traveling upwards of 150 miles per hour, this irresistible force finally met an immovable object.

There's an old African tribal poem that speaks of how our ancient ancestors dealt with the loss of their loved ones. It goes like this:

> Those who are dead are never gone:
> They are in the thickening shadow.
> The dead are not under the earth:
> They are in the tree that rustles,
> They are in the wood that groans,
> They are in the water that runs,
> They are in the water that sleeps,
> They are in the hut, they are in the crowd:
> The dead are not dead.

Earnhardt ran only one race in 2001, but his presence haunted the entire thirty-six-event season, from the first contest at Daytona where he was killed to the last race at New Hampshire, originally scheduled for the Sunday after September 11 but postponed to November 23 after the world went to hell and back in about the time it takes to watch a five-hundred-mile race.

At the time of his death, Dale was running interference so his son Dale Jr. and Michael Waltrip, both driving cars owned by the elder Earnhardt, could jockey for stock car racing's biggest win. In a scene too dramatic even for Hollywood, Waltrip took the checkered flag half a car length ahead of Junior and half a straightaway past Earnhardt's mangled Chevy.

One week later, my younger brother and I met at Rockingham to mourn our loss, and we were comforted beyond words to watch Steve Park, piloting another of Earnhardt's race cars, drive to victory in the Dura Lube 400. Two weeks later, Kevin Harvick, the rookie driver who took over Earnhardt's ride (minus the trademark #3, painted over with Harvick's #29), pulled into Victory Lane in Atlanta's Cracker Barrel 500.

It got better: At the second Daytona race, the Pepsi 400 held on my brother's birthday, July 7, Dale Jr. and Waltrip played hopscotch, Little E crossing the finish line just ahead of his teammate. After the traditional victory lap, they both spun doughnuts in the infield grass and climbed out of their steaming cars to share hugs and high fives. We watched the race at my father's, and at the end there wasn't a dry eye in the house. I stepped out into the warm summer night, and the moon hung silent in the distance as I shot bottle rockets off Dad's deck and watched them blaze up, pop, and disappear down the dark valley below.

The very next week, Harvick again drove Dale's car to victory at Chicago's Tropicana 400. As if that wasn't enough, Junior took two more races. On September 23 he won the Dover Downs MBNA.com 400, and on October 21 he grabbed what might have been the sweetest prize of all: the EA Sports 500 at Talladega, the fastest track on the circuit and also the last race his father ever won.

The specter of Earnhardt was not always a friendly ghost. Steve Park hit the wall in a Busch Series race at Darlington in August, and when rescue crews covered the wreckage with a huge blue tarp while they cut him out of the car, that old bastard Death reared his ugly head again. But Park survived the crash and, after rehab, raced again the next year.

Perhaps the most certain evidence of Earnhardt's continuing presence was a stunt pulled by Robby Gordon, the young upstart who took over as Harvick's teammate in 2001. In the last race of the year Jeff Gordon, Earnhardt's nemesis who became his good friend, had already wrapped up the season championship and was leading in the final laps. The other Gordon, Robby—no relation—slipped up behind him and, in true Intimidator style, tapped his rear fender and spun him out. The usually unflappable Jeff, an outspoken Christian, was so mad he later rammed Robby's car from behind. So much for turning the other cheek—or fender, as the case may be. After years of swapping metal with Earnhardt, Jeff Gordon must have felt haunted indeed.

They say you don't appreciate something until it's gone. My struggle all during the 2001 racing season was to keep up interest in a sport that, in a single grinding instant, had lost its main draw. In one of life's strange twists I recalled watching my own grandfather weather a similar storm after his favorite driver, Fireball Roberts, finally gave up the ghost a few days after a nasty wreck at Charlotte back in the 1960s.

After Dale died, racing sure as hell wasn't the same—not even close—but week after week I witnessed his legacy coming into its own. After all was said and done, NASCAR held its annual awards banquet at New York's cushy Waldorf Astoria hotel, and both Earnhardt Jr. and Harvick, who was voted Rookie of the Year, sat at the table reserved for the season's top-ten drivers, tuxedoed good ol' boys basking in the big-city spotlight. It was a spectacle my grandmother would have called "country come to town."

All ten award winners spoke of their admiration for Earnhardt and their grief over losing him. The champion Gordon, lately one of Earnhardt's paint-scraping rivals, recalled their friendship and the many things he had learned from this mentor both on and off the track. He also spoke of seeing the incredible devastation on his recent visit to Ground Zero, and called to mind the police and firefighters who had sacrificed their lives on that killing floor.

"Garthzilla" Brooks sang his megahit "The Dance" as a tribute to Earnhardt, and though this pop-country superstar leaves my ears cold, his words struck a nerve that connects both my smaller and our larger griefs:

And now I'm glad I didn't know
The way it all would end
The way it all would go.
Our lives are better left to chance.
I could have missed the pain
But I'd've had to miss the dance.

Who could have imagined twenty years ago that stock car racing and country music would take over the world? As my grandmother also said, "If you live long enough, you're liable to see just about anything." Indeed. Men skipping across the surface of the moon like little girls playing, the Berlin Wall falling like the fortified city of Jericho, hijacked airliners firebombing skyscrapers, our own Towers of Babel come a-tumblin' down—just about anything.

The most touching tribute of the evening was the appearance of Earnhardt's widow, Teresa, who has all but disappeared from public view since his death. After a standing ovation, with a trembling voice she accepted in her late husband's absence an award the ornery driver might never have won had he lived to see retirement: Most Popular Driver. It blessed my heart to see that Teresa had somehow found her smile.

When Dale Jr. stood to receive his Top Ten Driver award, with that blond hair, granite jaw, and Cheshire Cat grin, he was the spitting image of his daddy. Conjuring up both the humility and the indomitable spirit of Big E, Junior said, "When I reflect on the past season, I feel both grief and happiness. Losing my father was difficult, but I feel confident moving into the future. I've missed my father's approval very much, but one day soon my team will headline this joint."

At the Darlington race just nine days prior to the terrorist attacks in September, I took off my ball cap and covered my heart as I stood before one of the signs hung in an inconspicuous corner of the infield. The metal placards commemorate those drivers who have won at the infamous Track Too Tough to Tame, a site I've loved since I saw my first race there when I was nine years old, now hallowed ground. The sign read, "Darlington Winner's Alley: Dale Earnhardt," and listed his nine victories. In my mind's eye, I saw one of the things I liked and miss most about Dale: his moustache, half hiding that sweet, cocky smile. Somehow the bristly caterpillar across his upper lip reminds me he was a man, by turns foolish and inspiring, intimidating and generous.

How could anyone so alive, so full of piss and vinegar, just up and disappear? I don't know, but that old scientist and mystic Albert Einstein—a wizard walking the Earth if ever there was one—has said no energy is ever lost. Dale Earnhardt's death has changed me, as so many of us have been altered forever by the events of 9/11. It's the kind of personal transformation Pastor Hayne Rivers, the Baptist preacher of my childhood and the holiest man I ever knew until God took him, used to talk about every Sunday: the outer fruits of an inner revolution. As Jesus said and showed so well, what we say and do is a mirror reflection of who we really are deep down in our souls.

Ever since February 2001, and especially after September 11 of that same year, I'd like to think I take fewer things for granted, especially the folks I love and who love me. I try to listen a little more attentively to what others say and how they say it. I take closer note of the fear and hope in their eyes, and I'm a bit more willing to shake a hand and to give and receive a hug. Maybe most important of all, I find deep comfort in the knowledge that those who have gone on before, who no longer walk this good Earth, are still in a very real sense here with us. Whenever we pause to remember them and take to heart what all they meant to us and the things they taught us, we draw strength from their continued company and know their presence in ways we never could while they were still confined within their bodies.

The dead are not dead.